# Ready, Set, Go!

Ready, Set, Go!
*From Grind To Glory: The Justin Gatlin Story*

Justin Gatlin

©2024 All Rights Reserved. No portion of this book may be reproduced, stored in a retrieval system, or transmitted in any form or by any means- electronic, mechanical, photocopy, recording, scanning, or other-except for brief quotations in critical reviews or articles without the prior permission of the author.

Published by Game Changer Publishing

Paperback ISBN: 978-1-963793-62-8
Hardcover ISBN: 978-1-963793-63-5
Digital: ISBN: 978-1-963793-64-2

www.GameChangerPublishing.com

# DEDICATION

*I am dedicating this book to my family, friends, coaches and all of those who have helped me discover me. I thank you so much!*

*Justin*

**Scan the QR Code Below and Lets Connect!**

# Ready, Set, Go!

*From Grind to Glory: The Justin Gatlin Story*

Justin Gatlin

GAME CHANGER PUBLISHING

www.GameChangerPublishing.com

# Foreword

Every person is born with several natural gifts, such as intelligence, athleticism, musical and artistic abilities, and more. However, the key to maximizing those gifts is to apply challenging standards, mental toughness, and countless hours of focused work and refinements to become the best at what you do and, in some cases, the best in the world.

That's exactly how my friend, Justin Gatlin, has approached life to become one of the world's fastest humans on some of the biggest stages in the world.

Justin's athletic championship DNA is greatly enhanced by his discipline, determination, and resilience. He used these tools to find success as an elite athlete and continues to use them as he moves into the next phase of his life as a coach and mentor.

If you're not yet an elite performer like Justin, you may not fully understand the sacrifices involved in foregoing easier paths and instead dedicating yourself wholly to your passion. Nobody can teach you discipline or determination. They come from within. You simply must want something above all else and set aside distractions as you strive, often for years, to become the best in the world.

Many people I work with have these qualities. However, what sets Justin and others like him apart is resilience. There will be setbacks, failures, and doubts along the way. That is simply the way of the world when you take on life's biggest goals. But Justin learned long ago that resilience must be part of any standard you set, and he has called upon that character trait many times in his journey.

Discipline, determination, and resilience are all part of a larger champion mindset. As you'll read in *Ready, Set, Go!* Justin combines these with honesty, accountability, and grit to create the competitive advantage required to turn a championship mindset into championship outcomes.

I am such a believer in Justin and his methods that I asked him to train my daughter, Kennedy, who has shown an interest in running track. After several months with Justin's help, she recently ran an undefeated season in the 100m dash, which also just happened to be Justin's marquee event throughout his career. Justin has always been a gentleman, but he is also someone I consider a close friend, family mentor, and champion in every sense of the word.

It's time for you to read *Ready, Set, Go!* Step up to the starting line, set your feet in the starting blocks, listen for the sound of the starter's pistol, and get ready to learn valuable lessons that will help you cross the finish line first in any race you run.

Like Justin Gatlin, there can be no holding back if you want to become a champion in your life. Lean into every race you run with everything you've got.

It's your time.

And to that, I say, *"Ready, Set, Go!"*

— Ben Newman
 USA Today Top 5 Performance Coach
 2x Wall Street Journal Bestseller

# Table of Contents

Introduction ................................................................................... 1

Chapter 1 – Birth of Speed: Part 1 ................................................. 3

Chapter 2 – Birth of Speed: Part 2 ................................................. 9

Chapter 3 – Birth of Speed: Part 3 ............................................... 15

Chapter 4 – Birth of Speed: Part 4 ............................................... 27

Chapter 5 – Birth of Speed: Part 5 ............................................... 35

Chapter 6 – Forging a Champion: Part 1 ..................................... 41

Chapter 7 – Forging a Champion: Part 2 ..................................... 49

Chapter 8 – My Mount Everest: Part 1 ........................................ 57

Chapter 9 – My Mount Everest: Part 2 ........................................ 71

Chapter 10 – Purgatory: Part 1 .................................................... 83

Chapter 11 – Purgatory: Part 2 .................................................... 87

Chapter 12 – Purgatory: Part 3 .................................................... 95

Chapter 13 – Purgatory: Part 4 .................................................. 103

Chapter 14 – Feather of a Phoenix: Part 1 ................................. 111

Chapter 15 – Feather of a Phoenix: Part 2 ................................. 115

Chapter 16 – Feather of a Phoenix: Part 3 ................................. 119

Chapter 17 – Feather of a Phoenix: Part 4 ................................. 125

Chapter 18 – Body Over Mind: Part 1 ....................................... 131

Chapter 19 – Body Over Mind: Part 2 ....................................... 135

Chapter 20 – Body Over Mind: Part 3 ........................................................... 141

Chapter 21 – Climbing Mount Everest Twice: Part 1 ................................. 149

Chapter 22 – Climbing Mount Everest Twice: Part 2 ................................. 157

Chapter 23 – The Swan Song: Part 1 ............................................................ 165

Chapter 24 – The Swan Song: Part 2 ............................................................ 169

Chapter 25 – The Swan Song: Part 3 ............................................................ 173

Chapter 26 – The Swan Song: Part 4 ............................................................ 177

Chapter 27 – The Swan Song: Part 5 ............................................................ 181

Conclusion ......................................................................................................... 187

Afterword – A Letter to the Parents of a Gifted Child ................................ 189

Ready, Set, Go!
*From Grind To Glory: The Justin Gatlin Story*

Justin Gatlin

©2024 All Rights Reserved. No portion of this book may be reproduced, stored in a retrieval system, or transmitted in any form or by any means- electronic, mechanical, photocopy, recording, scanning, or other-except for brief quotations in critical reviews or articles without the prior permission of the author.

Published by Game Changer Publishing

Paperback ISBN: 978-1-963793-62-8
Hardcover ISBN: 978-1-963793-63-5
Digital: ISBN: 978-1-963793-64-2

www.GameChangerPublishing.com

# Introduction

My name is Justin Gatlin; that might ring a bell if you've followed the sprints at the Olympics. Yes, I'm that guy who's dashed past the blur of the track lines, feeling every heartbeat as if it's synced with the crowd's cheers. But beyond the medals and the podiums, I'm just a person who has faced as many hurdles off the track as on it.

It's been a long road filled with both incredible peaks and challenging valleys. My journey hasn't just been about training and talent; it's been about resilience, learning from failures, and keeping my eyes on the goal even when the finish line seemed out of reach.

I remember one rainy evening during a particularly tough training season. I was on the verge of giving up, feeling that perhaps my best days were behind me. That day, a conversation changed everything. My coach handed me an old photograph of my first race. Looking at that young, determined face, I remembered why I started running in the first place. That memory reignited a spark in me, and I decided to push through, leading to yet another comeback.

Throughout my career, many have asked how I've managed to stay at the top in such a demanding sport. This book is my way of answering that question. It's not just my story; it's a collection of lessons that I believe can inspire and guide anyone, regardless of their field.

This book is for the dreamers, the aspiring athletes, and anyone who's ever faced a challenge and wondered if they could overcome it. It's for parents, coaches, and mentors who help shape the future of young hopefuls.

From detailed training regimens to mental resilience strategies, I share insights that go beyond athletics. You'll get a behind-the-scenes look at the highs and lows of a professional sports career, along with practical advice that applies to any area of life. There are also words of wisdom from my parents on how they navigated the challenges of raising a talented athlete.

I hope that by turning the last page, you'll feel empowered to chase your own version of gold. Whether it's on the track, in the office, or in another walk of life, I want to pass on the baton of belief—that no matter the odds, you have the strength to overcome and succeed.

Thank you for picking up this book. Let's start this race together. Ready, set, go!

— Justin Gatlin

CHAPTER 1

# Birth of Speed: Part 1

I was born on February 10, 1982, in Brooklyn, New York. My earliest memories are of thinking of myself as a young athlete, though I didn't even know what athletics or sports were at the time.

On the playground, I found ways to compete against other kids: who could swing higher, who could climb the monkey bars faster, who could jump the farthest.

In hindsight, I showed signs of athleticism at an early age. I raced the kids in the neighborhood and soon found I was the fastest kid on the block. Then, at the age of six, I found out from my father that we were moving to Pensacola, Florida.

The South was extremely different from Brooklyn, New York. There were bugs I'd never seen before, the air had a different smell, and I was in awe of all of the trees around us. My mind raced with curiosity, and I wanted to run around and play on everything.

I believe that if we had stayed in New York, I would have still been an athlete, but I would have been a different kind of athlete. Maybe I would have played basketball. But moving to Pensacola helped me stretch my legs. It helped me find new adventures and meet new kids once we moved into our house. Then the physical challenge came along as kids tried to assert themselves. Everyone wanted to see who was the fastest or the strongest, and my athleticism shone once again.

I was confident enough to go up to kids and say, "Hey, race me while you're on your bike and I'm still on foot." After I beat them, there was no question that I was the fastest and probably most athletic kid amongst my circle of friends.

As I grew into Pensacola and went to different schools, meeting different friends, I still had a lot of time on my hands, but I wasn't old enough to play other sports yet. In the South, football is huge, but my mother did not like the sport because of the injuries it caused. She kept me away from contact sports, even at a young age.

Basketball was my first sport. I started playing recreational basketball for the YMCA and loved it. I remember using my athleticism to run up and down the court on fast breaks, making layup after layup because no one could stop me and no one could keep up with me. I shone on the court, especially when I was focused and my game was on. I joined the basketball team every year because I was hungry for friendship and competition.

But basketball wasn't my only extracurricular activity. I also played the piano, saxophone, and trumpet. These extracurricular activities were fun and challenging. I learned to play the piano from my aunt Marilyn, and My mother took me to lessons for the trumpet and saxophone.

Sometimes, these extracurricular activities were boring because I had to sit still. They also had a slow learning process, while I wanted to do everything fast, fast, fast. So, when I started doing other sports, it felt more natural.

In elementary school, one of my classmates was a kid named Billy Morris. Billy was what you would call a man-child. When we were in first grade, Billy had to be at least five foot eight, almost as tall as our teacher. They would look at each other eye to eye. The other kids were always scared of him because he was so big, but he was a really cool kid.

During recess every day, all the guys would get together, and we'd challenge each other to see who could jump the furthest, who was the fastest, and who was the best tag player. Often, we ended these challenges with a foot race.

We'd start at one place on the red clay track at Holmes Elementary and run to another point, just a straightaway, not all the way around the track. Little did I know that I was practicing track and field before I even knew what track and field was.

I raced Billy Morris every day, and nine times out of ten, he would beat me. But I would get better. I would get stronger. I would become more determined. Each time I raced him, I would think, *Okay, what is a good strategy to beat this kid? He has to be beatable.* Some days, he would be faster in the beginning or stronger at the end, and I would learn how to combat that.

Then it finally happened. I beat Billy Morris. It was a really close race. I guess you could say it was by a nose, but I finally edged him out.

Just like in my track and field professional career, when I competed against Usain Bolt, who would go on to win countless races. Then, when I needed my determination, my discipline, my confidence, and the hunger for competition that thrived inside of me, they would be used to help me win a championship and make history. I found that to be amazing as I got older.

Over the next few years, I discovered other sports. And, finally, I met track and field. I can't remember exactly what made me join the track team. Probably one of my friends, or even a coach, told me, "Hey, you're pretty fast. You should join the track team." You know, the usual conversation that directs people to a specific sport.

Track and field is not a very popular sport in America. Usually, fast kids or athletic kids are pushed towards basketball, football, or other popular sports. But I remember trying out for the track team. It was such an amazing experience. I looked around and thought, *Wait a minute. All these people are here to race or jump far?* I couldn't believe it. I had found a treasure trove of competition.

I had tried out for the track team without telling my parents. I still remember coming home with my jersey from Ferry Pass Middle School. It was this polyester old-school jersey, royal blue with white trim, and it said "Ferry Pass" across the front. But I brought it home with pride.

When I got home, my mom was sitting on the couch, watching some show, and my dad was at his computer, studying for his psychology degree. I walked in the door and said, "Guess what?"

"What?" they said casually. They weren't excited at all.

I showed them my jersey and told them I'd made the track team. My dad swiveled in his chair and looked at my mom. My mom looked at my dad, and then they both looked at me and burst out laughing. "What? You? Impossible. No way. This can't be happening. You are the slowest, laziest person we know."

# READY, SET, GO!

To their credit, what they said was true. I was lazy, slow to move, and slow to do my chores around the house. Their perception of me was that I didn't have any giddy-up and go, that I wasn't excited to do certain things. So, when they pulled me from the track team because of my grades, it made me more determined and hungry to get back out there.

I fell in love with just going to practice. I would get up every morning, go to school, and kind of blow through classes, waiting for track practice to start because that was the peak of my day. I loved it. I loved interacting with the people on the track team and watching them compete.

I got so enthralled in being a part of the track team and competing that my grades slipped. Not enough to kick me off the track team, but the coach would tell me, "Hey, you need to get your grades up."

My parents, though, had set a standard for me to live by. They didn't want me to have a mediocre education. They wanted me to be a success. So, when my grades slipped, my parents noticed and took me off the track team.

The next season, I was able to join the track team again, and this time, I was ready. My grades were good. I was meeting the challenge and was excited to be back out there. But now there was a new level of competition that I had never seen before: Sam Watts and Paul Lawrence. Sam went to Brown Barge, and Paul went to Warrington.

Sam was the slower of the two, but they both were faster than me, and I'd never encountered people who were so much stronger and faster than me. They beat me outright. It wasn't shoulder to shoulder. It wasn't a lean to the finish line. I was looking at the backs of their jerseys. This was a new experience for me, and it puzzled me.

I trained hard, and eventually, the same thing that happened with Billy Morris happened with Sam. I beat him. All the kids on my track team said, "What? That's crazy." No one had ever beaten Sam except for Paul.

Paul was strong and fast, but he also was very much a showman. He would walk onto the track with a female teammate on each arm. He would strut like he was the man because he believed he was the man.

When he ran, he got out fast and strong, and once he took off, there was no stopping him. If you couldn't keep up with his acceleration, you were left in his dust. I would watch the back of his jersey and the bottom of his feet pull away from me before he floated across the finish line. Those memories are forever seared into my mind.

Paul was really good in the long jump as well, which was another event that I loved. Once again, he was better than me. But I honored that. I respected that.

A lot of people become very frustrated when they encounter people who are better than them at something that they love. In my case, it inspired me to work harder, to keep going, to want to run faster. Throughout my middle school career, I never beat Paul. He was always the man.

CHAPTER 2

# Birth of Speed: Part 2

After graduating from middle school, I wanted to go to the high school my classmates were going to. Unfortunately, I lived on the border of the districts for Woodham High School and Booker T. Washington High School. By "border," I mean that I lived on the edge of the district for Woodham High School. It was a five- to six-mile drive to get there, and even longer by school bus, but I only lived a mile away from Washington.

My mom and dad had to write a letter to the school board in Tallahassee, two and a half hours away. It said, "Our son would love to go to this school. These are the reasons…"

Thankfully, I ended up getting what I wanted and went to Washington High School for my freshman and sophomore year. I really enjoyed it, and I still remember my friends. I even joined the swim team.

I couldn't comprehend the fact that I was swimming. When I got tired, I couldn't hang on the ropes. This was new to me because, in track and field, if you get tired, you can always just pull off to the side or kind of stride off into the infield to catch your breath—not in swimming. You're in the water. If you get tired, you have to swim to the other side. I wasn't feeling that at all. Eventually, I drifted away from the sport.

I decided to go out for the football team, and my mom was completely against it. She said, "You can play football all you want, but I'm never dropping you off. I'm never picking you up from practice or a game."

"Okay," I said. "I'm still gonna try out."

And I did. I was a freshman and one of the scrawniest guys on the team. Another kid was just as skinny as me. His name was Justin, too. We both had a love for football and bonding with our friends, but we didn't realize what our talent was in football. We were still trying to discover ourselves.

That year, I played defense instead of offense. I didn't understand route running or how to catch the ball properly, so the freshman football coach put me and the other Justin at the defensive end positions.

If you watch football, you know that defensive ends are big and athletic. They not only have to be able to block but also get around defenders. There's a lot of pushing and shoving and moving and sliding to the side and trying to get over a defender who might be even bigger than you because they're blocking you from getting to the quarterback. So, being a defensive end was a challenge, but I realized that I wanted to be a part of this team, and wherever I was on the field, I was okay with it.

I was on the left side of the field, and the other Justin A on the right. The other teams would laugh at us when they saw us. "Those are your defensive ends, those two toothpicks?" But they didn't realize how fast we were. Being quick and agile, we were able to dodge and maneuver around those bigger linemen trying to block us and put pressure on the quarterback.

The coach even designed a play for us called the "rat trap." The two of us would come around simultaneously and try to sack the quarterback. We put a lot of pressure on teams that way, and we were successful.

In my sophomore year, I was moved to free safety. This allowed me to roam the open field and use my speed. I felt more comfortable in that position. I even made the first interception of the year. I was very excited about that and felt like I'd made a little bit of history. Then I realized I wasn't getting treated fairly. Though I was contributing to the team, I was being sidelined so a senior could have more playing time than me.

I couldn't understand that. *We're here to win*, I thought, *so we should put our best out there. The second-best player should come in only when they're needed.* But this situation was flipped. I was the best, but I was getting benched.

When I asked the head coach, Coach Berkowsky, for an explanation, he told me, "Well, he's a senior, and he needs to be able to get himself out there so he can go on to college."

Mind you, I was a sophomore in high school. I didn't understand the need to get exposure and playing time so you could get an opportunity to go to college. I just felt like I was being treated unfairly.

So, I quit the football team. When I went to the head coach's office to turn in my pads and helmet, he said, "Are you sure?"

"Yeah," I said. "I don't feel like I'm being used properly, and this is not working for me. I don't think I'm being treated fairly."

"You know," he said, "if you feel like you're not being treated fairly, then you have to be able to take yourself out of the situation."

So, he did believe in me, but I told him I was going to quit the football team anyway, and I explained to him exactly why. His reply was, "Well, son, you're making a big mistake, and I don't want you to regret that. You will be sorry for quitting the football team."

I remember thinking, *That's all you have to say to me? That's it?* As I walked out, I turned to him and said, "No, Coach, you're going to be sorry." That was the last time we spoke to each other.

Then I joined the track team, and I felt I was home again. I could run and compete, and I knew that the best would always come out on top. That's how track and field is constructed.

This time, I tried new things, like the high jump and hurdles, but I was still doing sprints. We had one coach, Coach Whiteside, who really connected with the kids. He helped athletes be the best versions of themselves to go out on the track and win, and he was very successful at that. Unfortunately, he was a distance coach and didn't have much input for a sprinter, hurdler, or jumper, all the things I was doing.

Our sprint and hurdle coach was the wide receiver coach for the football team. He didn't know much about track and field. On a lot of days, he would come out to track practice with his folding chair and his newspaper, and he would sit down, cross his legs, and do crossword puzzles. He was just kind of babysitting us, so we had to learn everything on our own. The assistant coaches and former students would help us out, but our coach only taught us the basics.

Once the season started, I was excited. On the sprinting side, I was a dark horse because I was faster than all the other varsity guys on the team. But I also did other events, which kept me from being a bona fide sprinter.

Because of this, everyone seemed to think my wins were a fluke for some time. When I won the district meet, a lot of my opponents were amazed, but they still seemed to say, "Eh, you got lucky." But I knew in my heart it was the start of something special.

I did hurdles, too. Hurdles were really complex, which excited me. The thing about hurdles is that it has so many layers of competition.

You're racing against time, you're racing against seven other athletes, and you're trying to run as fast as you can and get over ten barriers at the same time.

It was like organized chaos, but I loved it because it made me dial in and focus. It required me to be athletic and competitive. I also had to know how to operate and move precisely to be faster than the guys next to me. That's what it came down to—being the best hurdler meant having better mechanics than everyone else. That was something that got away from me because I always just wanted to compete.

There was an athlete named AJ who ran for Woodham High School, where I was supposed to go to school. AJ always beat me in hurdles because he had better mechanics than me, but I knew I could beat him in a flat-out race by far. He was graceful and had a great lead leg. He'd also snap his trail leg down. When it came to hurdles, he just moved.

I always beat him between hurdles, so he never got too far ahead of me. He'd gain distance on me at the hurdle, I would almost always catch him, and then I'd fall behind again going over the next hurdle. It was frustrating, but I was hungry to learn more.

After one meet, guess who walked over and tapped me on the shoulder? The Woodham boys track team head coach. His name was Coach Cormier. "Hey," he said, "I see you over there hurdling for Washington. You're pretty good. But you could be way better. I want to introduce you to the hurdle coach over at Woodham."

He introduced me to Coach TJ Rollins, who said, "You have real talent. You just don't know what you're doing." They both laughed at me.

"Well," I said, "I need to know what I'm doing because I want to be the best I can be." They looked at each other when I said that because they had never heard such a young athlete speak in that manner.

"Where do you live?" said Coach Cormier. When I told him, he replied, "If you get an opportunity to transfer to our school, we'll be able to help you more." That was the end of the conversation, but as the summer went on, we interacted here and there.

Another guy on my team was a kid named Crandon Sellers. Crandon was fast, and I'd known him since the first grade. He was the kid who sat next to the teacher, not because he was the teacher's pet but because he was so disruptive. Crandon was the only guy on the team that I felt was a threat. When we raced, it was always a very close finish.

Crandon was also thinking about transferring to a better school so he could learn to run faster and have better opportunities. So, we talked and thought about it through the summer.

When I told my mom and dad, they said, "Well, you are supposed to go to Woodham. You're in the Woodham district." They had a conversation with Coach Cormier, who told them, "This will be easy. Just do this, this, and this, and Justin will be back at our school where he's supposed to be." And that's what they did. At the start of my junior year, I transferred to Woodham High School. It turned out to be one of the best decisions I ever made.

When my parents met with Coach Cormier, he said, "Academically, Justin's not even on track to go to college." Like I said earlier, my parents were all about academics, so when they heard that, they realized they needed to make a change. Now, not only was I getting the best coaching, but I was also getting the best teaching.

CHAPTER 3

# Birth of Speed: Part 3

Woodham was a totally different environment than Washington. The kids were different, and so was the building. It was more open, with a big courtyard in the middle. It almost felt like college, where you had to walk across campus to get to class, and it felt pretty cool.

Once I met the track kids at Woodham, I knew I belonged there. The girls' track team was probably better than the boys' team. Paul Bryant was the head coach for the girls, and he kept them in line. They were regimented and competed at a high level, pretty much winning every track meet they went to. The Woodham track girls dominated the local, district, and regional meets, and they went to state every year.

As for the boys' side, Sam Watts, Paul Lawrence, Alan Cotton, Mario Purifoy, Sean Cunningham, Mario Hooper, Ellis Dubrow, and I, along with so many other great athletes, were a part of a super team. The team was so good that we'd tell each other, "Man, if we don't win state, we don't deserve to run track." We created a brotherhood, a bond. It was a moment I'll never forget. We were a dominant force, winning every event.

Backtracking just a bit, before I left Washington, I would go on trips with the team. My mom was always health conscious. Instead of junk food and sodas, she would put juice in a huge Thermos for me. Looking back now, it was very geeky, but I was all about staying healthy and not getting cramps and things like that.

One time, we were on a road trip to a track meet, and one of my teammates asked me, "What's in your Thermos? You always have it with you."

"It's juice," I said matter-of-factly.

"Juice?" he said. "What? You got juice? Apple juice?"

"Yeah," I replied. "You know, cran-apple juice, apple juice, sometimes grape juice, whatever. Juice."

We hadn't been in athletics for very long, so we had no idea what Gatorade was. I don't think we could have even afforded it. Gatorade was a premium beverage to have. The kids started low-key teasing me, saying things like, "Man, this dude out here drinking juice. All right, Juice Man." That's what they would call me: "Juice Man."

When I started running faster and became the district champion, their tone changed. "Whoa, he's real. That's Juice Man. He's Juice." Every time I ran, they'd say, "Oh, he's about to unlock the juice," and they would chant, "Juice, Juice, Juice, Juice, Juice." I went from being "Juice Man" to just "Juice."

This nickname stuck with me, even through college. There are still people throughout Pensacola who only know me as Juice. In fact, if I were to call up my college coach right now, he'd say, "Hey, what's up Juice?"

The name became very popular. When I was in high school, my parents allowed me to get a tattoo, and it was the word "Juice," along with a track shoe. I thought I was a real badass.

Once I got on the powerhouse team at Woodham High School, it felt like I was on the Chicago Bulls. And Coach Rollins and Coach Cormier were the coaches. They realized that not only did we have athletes who could run and win races, we had athletes who could score points. In track, points are the name of the game. When an athlete wins first place in any event, it adds 10 points to their team score (Second Place: 8 points, Third Place: 6 points—all the way down to 1 point for Eighth Place).

Being very athletic and talented, I was able to compete in the long jump. I was often jumping 24 feet, 11 inches. Only one guy was a better long jumper than me, and he only beat me by about an inch. So, it was a given that we would be winning points in the event if I were competing.

I was also a hurdler: 110-meter hurdles and 300-meter hurdles, and I was getting really good at both events, to the point where I was state champion in my junior year.

But I was missing out when it came to the sprinting side because we had eight sprinters on our team, enough to make two 4x100 relay teams. Of course, we couldn't make two relay teams, so now we were looking at a situation where some guys would compete but wouldn't be able to score points for our team because they wouldn't be able to place.

The coaches realized that having me in the sprints, even though I would win and score points for us, would take away the opportunity for other guys on the team to score points for us, too. So, I didn't run the sprints that much during my junior year. I was basically the hurdler, the jumper, and the anchor leg on the 4x100.

We went on to dominate that season and made it to state, but there we got second, which was crazy because our team should have won. What happened was that too many of our teammates realized how good we were and just settled. They became complacent and slacked off in practice or preparation for competition. There were even whispers of teammates who were hung over while competing, which is crazy, but we still got second.

The ride home for us was a mixed bag of emotions because the girls' track team won. They had dominated the whole year, and we were supposed to win, too. The coaches would separate us on the bus, so one side would be girls, and one side would be guys. Of course, the girls were happy, but the guys were really sad because we should have gotten first place.

Going into my senior year, there was a big transfer of responsibility because most of the sprinters graduated. Only Sean Cunningham, Crandon Sellers, Sam Watts, and I remained. Sam moved, and he left the team as well. So, we didn't have that many sprinters, just enough to make a 4x100 team.

Senior year was a time for me to become a leader—and that meant not leading by words but by example. I had to get out there and compete. I came through and dominated the hurdles. The coaches finally allowed me to sprint, so I started dominating those events, too.

I was becoming known nationally. I discovered this when I went to the Meet of Champions in Mobile, Alabama. The other competitors were athletes from that region of the country, guys from Mississippi, Alabama, maybe Georgia, Florida, and even as far as Louisiana. These were elite athletes, many of them the best in the nation.

I met a guy from Tupelo, Mississippi. His name was Deandre' Eiland, and he was super talented in the hurdles, maybe top three in the nation in the 110 hurdles and top two, if not number one, in the 300 hurdles. He went on to win the 110 hurdles that day. It was close—I was maybe a shoulder length away from him when he won. I think that surprised him because he didn't even know who I was. I didn't feel down or frustrated at the loss; I just knew that I'd wanted that win. It should have been my win.

Coach Cormier came over to me, grabbed me by my shoulders, and did what he was so good at doing. He spoke life *into* me. He spoke athleticism *into* me. That is something that I loved about Coach Cormier.

He didn't have to be the coach who showed you the form and the technique, but he was the coach who would say, "This is what you can do." Coach Cormier was the first coach to ever tell me I was a world-class athlete, and he told me in high school, before I even knew what a world-class athlete was.

Coach Cormier grabbed me by my shoulders and said, "Hey, you're going to PR today in the 300 hurdles. Don't worry about that 110-hurdle race. Ready to run fast?"

He gave me a time, and I said, "Coach, I've never had that time before."

"I know," he said, "but you're ready, and you're world-class, and that's what you're going to do today."

When he said that to me, I didn't want to do anything less. I didn't question it. He gave me a pat on the back and said, "Go out there and get it done."

We got on the blocks, and I looked at Eiland. He had a confident look on his face because this was his groove. He was a good short hurdler, but he was a better long hurdler. The starter said, "Set," and the gun went off, *Pow*. I ran like a bat out of hell, clearing hurdles, going, going, going.

I ran so hard that he never gained any ground on me. Throughout the race, I never saw him.

When I came across the line, I'd run a time even better than what my coach had said I would because I was so determined and believed that I was a world-class athlete, whatever that was. I knew that I had a standard to live up to, and that meant winning this race, so that was what I went on to do.

At that meet, there was a guy named Casey Combest. He had been dubbed the fastest kid in the nation. I was running a 10.4 in the 100 at that point, but he was running a 10.1. Now, the difference between our times was quicker than a finger snap, but in track and field, that's an immense gap. I watched him run from the stands because I had only been invited for the hurdles. All the kids were saying, "He's here. He's at the track. He's here. He's here."

I could feel the nervous energy of all those kids, who were either excited to see him run or nervous about running against him. It was a weird energy, like his reputation had preceded him. That was the first time I'd seen someone strike both excitement and fear in his competitors and the audience.

Casey was a short white kid from Kentucky. He wasn't muscular—or even someone you would look at and say, "Hey, this guy is obviously better than everybody else." He was just a scrawny, quiet guy with a blonde buzz cut. I never saw him smile or say anything before getting in the blocks. And when the gun went off, he destroyed the whole field. There was no competition at all.

The clock stopped at 9.99. To run sub-10 is phenomenal. Professional athletes are waiting to run sub-10; let's just put it like that. This kid was still a high-schooler. His performance blew me away. He was a whole other level of athlete.

I became really curious after watching him run. I didn't have fear or anxiety like some of my teammates did. I wanted to test myself against someone like him. Thinking about it kept me up for days. *Wow*, I thought, *that guy was amazing.*

Even though I never got the opportunity to race against Casey, he inspired me to continue to dominate and to reach a new level of winning.

The next meet was at Woodham High School. The track there was different. You know how when you pull into a parking lot, like at a shopping center, and get out of the car and the lot's paved with asphalt? That was what our track was made of, that asphalt.

As kids, we idolized professional athletes. They wore spikes with metal teeth that you'd screw into the soles. We wanted to be just like the professionals, but they were running on rubber surfaces while we were running on asphalt. We still put the metal spikes on, and we would be skating all over the place on the asphalt, slipping and sliding while trying to run as fast as we could.

Why we didn't just put on regular lightweight racing flats was beyond me. I wish I could do that part over again, but at the same time, it was exciting to wear the same shoes as Maurice Green, Marion Jones, or Michael Johnson. We could say we were going to run just as fast as them.

I told myself, "One day, I'm going to have my own pair of shoes. I'm going to run that fast."

At that home meet, running on that asphalt, I competed in the 300 hurdles. One of the kids I trained with and who was competing in the hurdles with me wasn't a very good athlete. He was a walk-on who was just happy to be there. He liked running, wanted to have the fellowship of being on a team, and was going to try to do the best that he could. But he was very slow.

We lined up for the race, and the gun went off. I started jumping the hurdles, business as usual, dominating the race. There were only maybe six or seven guys in the race. From the stagger I was at, I saw this kid fall. When you fall on asphalt, you get bruises, rashes, and even blood. It was gnarly.

I turned around in the middle of the race, ran back to him, and said, "Hey, are you good? Are you okay?"

He was dazed and confused, not only from falling but also because I'd come back to help. He must have been thinking, *Why is Justin here when he should be running?*

I picked him up and said, "Come on, man. We've got to finish this race."

I don't know what made me do this. He wasn't one of my friends in school. He was just a teammate. But I just felt that as a leader, this was something I needed to do. But then I heard the coach yelling at me from the stands, "What are you doing?" I took off running and caught all of the other athletes who had passed me, and I still won that race.

Coach Cormier came over to me and said, "Congratulations on winning that race and becoming a very good humanitarian, but let's not do that ever again. That's not what we're here for. We're here to win."

Team camaraderie was everything to me. My teammates were the guys who cheered for me. They were the guys who congratulated me first, and when they did, I knew it was genuine because they saw how hard I worked, and I knew how hard they worked for their accomplishments. It was like a brotherhood: if you're down, I'm down. So, I wanted to make sure that my teammate was good.

Another situation happened before state. I was competing in the high jump, jumping almost six feet ten inches. For whatever reason, I was wearing spikes with metal teeth while running on asphalt. To make the jump over the bar, I had to make a sharp turn. And since I was left-handed, my approach was different from everybody else's because they were mostly right-handed.

The judge, who obviously worked at the rival school, stood on the asphalt only from the opposite side. This gave an advantage to everyone except for me. I asked him, "Can you sweep my side off?"

"You'll be fine," he said.

As I went for my jump, I slipped and fell. It happened so quickly that the next thing I knew, I was lying on my left side with my arm extended and my ear touching my shoulder. Everyone was gasping with shock.

When I got up, I was covered in bruises and cuts. I needed to get bandaged up. I really chewed out the judge to the point where he said, "Hey, you can't talk to me like that." My coach came over and apologized on my behalf for speaking to the line judge like that.

That episode put me in a weird state that day, where I wasn't just competing with happiness anymore. I had a fire in me now. I was angry. I was mad. And I felt embarrassed and wanted to fix the situation. I didn't want to be the kid walking around with white gauze all over his legs and arms, whom everyone's making fun of or pitying.

I was such a dominant force from that point on, beating everybody by far in every other event. I finally felt like I fought those hurdles, that I fought the 100 meters, and that I fought the long jump, and I won each and every one of them.

Then I went on to state. It was like déjà vu all over again. I felt like we weren't going to win state because now we'd only brought four athletes as opposed to the year before, when we'd brought half a busload of guys but still only got second.

We had a discus thrower named Doug Morris, the little brother of Billy Morris, whom I'd gone to elementary school with. We had a high jumper named Carl, and we had Crandon Sellers, who was competing in the 100 and the 200. Needless to say, this time, we weren't on a bus. Coach Cormier drove us in a minivan from Pensacola all the way to Gainesville, which was about a six-hour drive.

I don't think we had any intention of winning state that year. We just went out there to do the best we could. We didn't have a relay team, for one thing. To win at that level, you had to have a relay team to get enough points.

I had qualified for the high jump, the long jump, the 110 hurdles, the 300 hurdles, and the 100 meters and was almost maxed out on how many events I could do. I was pretty much always maxed out, though. I did all those events all the time, basically.

First, I did the long jump, and I scored big in the event. Next was the high jump, but my coach told me, "Let's not focus on the high jump. Instead, let's put our energy into the hurdles and sprints." So, I opted out. I didn't even compete in the event, even though I qualified for it. Carl, who was a high jumper for our team, went on to get second in the state, which was a shock to all of us because he wasn't the best high jumper, but he competed that day.

Carl's performance sparked inspiration in all of us. Doug Morris went out there and had the best showing he'd ever had, getting top five in the discus. Crandon got top three in the 200 and also placed in the 100.

This is where the magic happened for me. I won the 300 hurdles. Hands down, that was my event. No one could ever touch me in the 300 hurdles. Then I won the 110 hurdles, which was a competitive race. But the challenge was I had to run back over to the starting line immediately after winning the 110 hurdles to run the 100-meter state championship race.

I got on the podium, and my parents were there in the stands, and it was like everyone in the stands knew that I had signed up for all these races. Everyone was yelling, "Get off the podium! Go back to the starting line! They're about to start the 100 meters!"

So, I jumped off the podium before they could finish the medal ceremony and ran to the 100-meter starting line. Then I remembered I still had my medal on, so I took it off, asked one of my coaches to hold it, and then got in the blocks. Seconds later, the gun went off, and I won the 100 meters.

I'd just finished the 110 hurdles, so the other racers should have had an advantage over me, but I dominated that field once again. It was an exciting moment because I'd scored 36 of my team's 52 points. I was dubbed "the one-man army," which was nice, but my teammates also contributed. I couldn't have done it alone.

Then it came down to a relay. For us to win state by half a point, Lincoln High School had to lose the 4x400. I sat in the stands, watching Lincoln High School compete at the end of the meet. It was agonizing. The gun went off, and just like that, Lincoln came in second. We won state by half a point.

It was the most amazing situation that I've ever been in. I did everything I could do as an athlete—all of us did—and then we had to sit and wait for a team to fall for us to win. It was a confusing situation, but it was one I'll never forget. And I loved it.

I grabbed the trophy and hugged it like Michael Jordan. I look at that picture often. That was a time when I loved what I was doing.

CHAPTER 4

# Birth of Speed: Part 4

After our win at state, I had a better understanding of organized track and field, and I began to realize that there was a college level and a professional level to the sport. I became a student of the game and just loved the sport, period.

I dubbed myself Justin Greene, after Mo Greene, and Paul Lawrence, my best friend who would spend the night with me before track meets so we could go to them together, called himself Paul Drummond. He called himself that because there was an athlete named John Drummond who trained with Maurice Greene. So, he was like, "All right, Paul Drummond and Justin Greene. We're getting ready to go." That was our little inside joke.

During my senior year, I started to get letters from colleges that were looking at me. Weirdly enough, I didn't play football in my junior or senior year of high school because Coach Cormier told me, "That's not your road. You are a sprinter, a world-class athlete. Football's only going to hold you back."

I know that made the Woodham football coach, Coach Sherrill, a little sad because he wanted to get his hands on me so I could run those goal routes, catch the ball, and outrun everybody on the field. He was in such awe of me as an athlete that he wanted to test my 40-yard time while I was in high school. So, he pulled me out of class one day and brought me over to the track.

"Alright, man, we know you're fast. How fast are you for real? I'm going to time you on the 40 yards. What do you think you can run?"

"I don't know," I said. "I've never been timed running 40 yards. I don't know what that means."

"You're going to start here, and you're going to go," he said. "And I'm going to time you when you move."

I got in my running stance, and once I moved, he pushed the button on the hand clock, and I ran. I zoomed right past him as fast as I could, and he looked at the clock and couldn't believe what he saw. I didn't know what it meant. He scratched his head a little bit and said, "My thumb might be off a little bit. Maybe you want to run it again?"

"Yeah," I said. "I'll run it again." I was all about competition and running fast. I loved it.

This time, he said, "You know what? I'm going to say, 'Ready, set, go,' because you're used to that."

So, he said, "Ready, set, go." I ran as fast as I could, and when I passed him, he stopped the clock. He looked at it again and scratched his head even more.

"I don't understand what's going on," he said.

"What do you mean?" I asked. "What's happening?"

"First, you ran a 4.28. Then you ran a 4.29."

"What does that even mean?" I asked.

"That means you're extremely fast."

"I know that, Coach. I'm a state champ, two years in a row."

"I know," he said, "but that means you're fast. Like, even in the football world, you're fast."

Running a 4.2 as a professional athlete or a collegiate athlete training to go pro is a feat within itself. Only a handful of football players have ever run a 4.2. The record is 4.21, and it still stands today. So, to run a 4.29 and 4.28, even on a hand timer, was abnormal for a high school kid.

From that point on, Coach Sherrill was mesmerized by my speed. He started putting my name out there to colleges, like, "Hey, we got a fast kid who runs hurdles."

I was getting a letter from the University of Clemson maybe once a week. I ended up with maybe 20-something letters from Clemson about football, football and track, or just track. They really wanted me badly.

I was getting letters from across the nation, from Florida, LSU, and even Ivy League schools like Brown. I was getting letters from Hawaii and UCLA. I was getting letters from everywhere. I was amazed that so many people recognized my talent. I didn't know these people even knew I existed, let alone wanted me to come to their school. It was an incredible experience.

LSU recruited me, and my parents said, "You can do these trips on one condition. You can only go to a school that is within driving distance from us, meaning we can get you within a day if we need to. So you have to be less than 12 hours away from us."

This upset me. I wanted to go to California and Hawaii. I wanted to experience the world. I don't think they even knew that, but I wanted to get as far from Pensacola as I could. Not because I wanted to be away from them but just to experience the world. It was already in me that I wanted to see what the world was made of.

The first trip I took was to LSU. I enjoyed that trip. It was an experience.

I was picked up by Pat Henry in his Jaguar, and he took me to a four-star hotel. This was the first time I'd ever stayed at a hotel by myself, let alone traveled by myself. It was amazing. Then he took me to eat lunch at his lake house.

My host, Derek Brew, was the fastest 400-meter runner in the world at the time. Even in college, his times were superior. And he was such a cool dude. He took me to a football game, and it started pouring down raining. We had to run across campus to get to the dorm of one of his girl teammates. Two or three of them were staying in the same dorm room.

When we got there, we were both drenched, and I was shivering. I was skin and bones, 160 pounds. Derek said, "Oh man, we've got to get you out of these wet clothes."

I went to one of their rooms, took off my clothes, and handed them through the crack of the door, and they washed and dried them for me to make sure I was warm. They were very hospitable, and from that point on, we had a good time.

I enjoyed LSU. Before leaving, I told Pat Henry, "I'm coming to your school. I love it here. You've got all the fast guys, you've got all the cute girls, and it seems like there's great competition. The food's amazing, too. I'm coming here."

Once I left LSU, in my mind, I was an LSU Tiger. But back home, my parents said, "You've got to take your other trips. You can't just take one trip. What are you doing?"

My second trip was to Tennessee. When I visited the campus, I had the total opposite time than at LSU. I didn't have a bad time; it was just a different experience. Coach Vince Anderson, the sprint coach there, picked me up in his Jeep. It wasn't raggedy, but you could tell it was a little beaten up. When I closed the door, the rear-view mirror fell off the windshield.

Coach Anderson was a great guy, and I enjoyed conversing with him. Then he pulled up to the dorm. Mind you, I had stayed in a hotel at LSU. At first, I thought, *All right, I'll stay in the dorm. I have no problem with this. I have to stay in the dorm if I come to college anyway.*

But when I got to the dorm room, it was just a big box. And then I discovered that I wouldn't even be staying in a bed; I would be sleeping on a cot in the corner. And that's where I stayed with two other athletes.

I met my host, and he was a good guy. But I could tell that there was a little bit of static between us because I was a young sprinter coming in who was good and he was already sprinting on the team but was on his way out. I would be coming in during his last year.

He took me to a party and left me there. "Hey, man," he said. "I'm out."

"All right, cool," I said. "I'm having a good time hanging out."

"Well, I'm gone," he said, and then he just left me.

No problem. I made friends on campus, and we stayed up all night. We talked and had fun.

I went to the football game the next day, and it was amazing. Watching the Tennessee Vols run out onto the field and hearing "Rocky Top" play for the first time was an amazing experience.

I got to meet and hang out with a lot of the track guys on the team, D-Bell, Carl, Rocky, Cameron, Hassan, and they showed me around. We had a great time. It just was a good bonding experience.

Once I got back home, I realized that the trips had been polar opposites. One was selling me on all the things that they had there, and one was selling me on who they were as a team, as an organization, and what they were all about.

The coach at Tennessee had said, "I can't promise you a championship, but I can promise you that I can help make you the best athlete you want to be." That resonated with me so much that I said, "I'm sold, Coach. Let's do this."

I made an adult decision. When I returned home, I told my parents how I'd had a good time, but if I went to LSU, I wouldn't be riding around in a Jaguar or staying in any hotel. And who was to say any of the cute girls who washed my clothes were going to even like me when I got there? I was going to go somewhere I knew I could make a name for myself and build a legacy, where I could work with guys who were hungry to be the best. I decided to go to Tennessee.

I asked my mom, "Can you call Coach Pat Henry and tell him that I'm decommitting?"

She looked at me and said, "No, that's your job. You made that decision. You got yourself into that. You've got to get yourself out of it."

I picked up the phone and called Coach Henry, telling him in a very nervous way that I had decided not to go to LSU. He was upset. Obviously, he did not show just how upset he was, but he was upset enough for me to notice it. For the next two years, he didn't talk to me. Even if he walked past me and our shoulders brushed, he acted like I didn't exist. But from that point on, I began to bond with Coach Anderson from Tennessee.

CHAPTER 5

# Birth of Speed: Part 5

I went to Kissimmee for a summer race, the first time I'd ever gotten to do one. Then I went down to the Junior Olympics and signed up to do the short hurdles. I looked over my dad's shoulder while he registered me, and the form asked for an age group. At that time, my age group was 14 to 15. The rest were 16 to 17.

I told my dad, "Sign me up with the older kids." He looked at me like I was crazy, so I said, "I want the challenge. I know I can beat the kids my age. I want to see how good I am against older kids." So, he signed me up

My mom had a fit about it. "We came down here all the way from Pensacola (basically a seven-hour drive), and he signed up for the wrong age group. Why is he doing this? What is he doing?"

My dad said, "He wants to test himself. He wants to see how good he is."

I vividly remember watching the other kids in the race with me while they were warming up. Wow, they were amazing. When the gun went off, I just remember wanting to compete, compete, compete at a high level. And I recalled all the cues Coach Rollins told me I needed to do. And when the smoke cleared, I got third. Only two kids in the older age group were faster than me.

That was such an eye-opening moment for me, the realization that it wasn't about age. It was about hunger. Just because someone was older than me, it didn't mean they were better than me. From that moment on, I didn't fear running against anybody at any age. No matter who my competitors were, I was going to put my best foot forward.

My next meet was High School Nationals in Raleigh-Durham, North Carolina. I was so excited to go to nationals for the first time as a junior. But when I tried to sign up for the 300-meter hurdles, I could not find it on the list. I soon discovered that there was no 300-meter hurdles race; there was only the 400-meter hurdles. I'd never run the 400-meter hurdles. In Florida, they only did the 300-meter hurdles. I asked Coach Cormier what I should do, and he said, "Try it out and see if you like it." So, I signed up.

I was so nervous. In the hotel room, in an early sign of how regimented and disciplined I would become, I called my coach and asked him about cues and tactics. "How am I going to get through this 400-meter-hurdle race? I've only competed in the 300-meter hurdles."

My coach did his best to walk me through the steps. Then I told him, "The hurdles are different. They're higher. What do I do?" He continued to calmly give me advice on what to do. He even told me what to eat. I took it all in.

Afterward, I told my parents, "You've got to take me to IHOP tomorrow, and we've got to get some steak and eggs. We've got to get some protein." I took control of how the trip was going to go, and they just kind of let me. Their attitude was, "This is your show, so what are you going to do?" So, we went through the whole regimen.

The day of the race, I was very nervous. I was competing in an event I'd never run before and was up against the best in the nation. When the gun went off, I took off. I competed hard for the first three hundred meters, and then I hit the wall. My body was not adapted to go beyond that with hurdles. At that point, I just tried to survive the race. I didn't win. I didn't even place. But I felt like I did. All I wanted was to make it across that finish line, and I did.

After the race, I stumbled onto the inner field and lay down on the grass, facing the sky. I lay there long enough for my mom to yell from the stands, "Justin, are you okay?" All I could do was throw my hand up and give her a thumbs-up. My body was in shock. That was my first experience at High School Nationals.

Fast-forward to my senior year. High School Nationals was in the same place, Raleigh-Durham, and I signed up for the meet. Even though I ran sprints, everyone knew me as a hurdler. I called the High School Nationals meet promoter and begged him, "Please, can I just race the 100? Can you put me in the 100 meters? I know I'm not the fastest kid in the nation when it comes to the 100 meters, but is there a way that you can take me from the hurdles and put me in the 100? I really want to run the 100 for the last race of my high school career."

This went on for a while, and finally, he said, "All right, Justin. I'll do this for you."

We went down to Raleigh-Durham, and I warmed up for the race. It was a who's who of the top kids in the nation. At the time, Dwight Thomas was the 100-meter phenom, the next version of Casey Combest. He was running 10.1 and 10.2 in the 100 meters. There was also a guy named Joey Porter, who was already signed up to go to Purdue for football. He was built like a running back and was super-fast.

I went through that gauntlet and made it from the prelims to the semis. I beat everybody in these rounds. In the finals, I lined up against Dwight and Joey, supposedly "the fastest kids in the nation."

I got into my set position and leaned back. I didn't know much about sprinting or proper technique. When the gun went off, I rocked forward.

I never caught Dwight or Joey. When we came across the line, Dwight was first with a time of 10.16. Joey Porter was next with a 10.26, and I finished with a time of 10.36. That was a new PR for me, and it made me the third-fastest kid in the nation. As I walked back down the track and across the field, I looked at the scoreboard, and my heart swelled with happiness and pride.

From the stands, someone said, "Hey, Justin." I looked up and saw bright orange hanging over the railing. It was Vince Anderson from Tennessee. He said, "I did not know you could sprint, my friend."

"Yeah," I said, "I like sprinting a lot. It's fun."

"Oh," he said, "we have something in store for you, then. You know what? Something you could fix right now is not rocking back in the blocks. If you hadn't rocked back, you might be looking at the silver medal right now."

"For real?" I said.

"Yeah," he replied. "That's the kind of thing I could teach you to help you become better. Remember this conversation."

That's what he said to me, and that's what I did. I remembered it.

So, I committed to the University of Tennessee. My high school campaign was officially done, but I was excited to start a new chapter: going to college.

### The Importance of Mindset

Mindset comes from a combination of Passion, Determination, Discipline and Balance. Passion is a healthy obsession where you know that on the other side, you will achieve your goals. It's the kind of obsession where you start to fall in love with the process more than the goal itself. It fuels your determination, even in moments or days that seem harder than normal. You have to create a level of obsession. A clear path isn't always as clear as we may think. Obstacles will test your desire to be determined. Discipline is the set structure and process that you follow every day, no matter what.

There will be days when you are tired and just don't feel like doing what needs to be done. Giving in to that leads to complacency and mediocrity. You have to work through those feelings, those difficult moments. Your discipline will also help you set a pace that evolves and transitions as you grow, where every step you achieve and work towards feels rewarding. Finally, Balance is important to the growth of your goal. Too little drive will slow your progression and you'll lose interest and focus on your goal. Too much drive can burn you out and leave you feeling overwhelmed. Find your "sweet spot."

---

To help you begin your journey to extraordinary success, I am listing below my **Top Three Actionable Steps** you can begin taking right now.

- Start off by identifying passion that you can grow into a clear path that can lead into a successful goal.
- Create discipline by turning your passion into a daily priority.
- Be determined to achieve your goals.

CHAPTER 6

# Forging a Champion: Part 1

My college coach, Vince Anderson, not only did a great job of teaching technique and race strategy, but he poured emotion into his athletes. As a one-on-one coach, he stands alone. The words he delivered to me as a coach made me feel more passionate about being a champion and a winner.

It started with Coach Cormier, my high school coach, who first told me I was a world champion. This led to Vince Anderson always saying, "You're the Michael Jordan of track and field. You're Wayne Gretzky. You're an athlete who stands alone through times when other athletes would crumble." Hearing those words always reinforced me, taking me to that next level so I could stay passionate about what I wanted to do as an athlete and the goals I wanted to achieve.

Whereas other coaches would just tell you what to do, Coach Anderson actually taught. He put together a binder that we athletes would study as if we were preparing for a test. He wanted us to think like professionals and not just operate as amateur athletes.

I remember stepping onto campus for our first days of practice at the University of Tennessee after getting the full scholarship. I had been recruited as a hurdler because that was what I was known for throughout high school, as a hurdler. So, the first practice I had was with the hurdles. I watched the older hurdlers, juniors and seniors, and they were gracefully gliding over the hurdles.

The hurdles were at a height that I was not used to. I was used to the high school height, which is 36 inches off the ground. Now I would be jumping over 42-inch hurdles. It was a whole different level of competition for me. I was already being challenged as the previous hurdle height was basically at my hips, while the new height was almost above my belly button.

The first time I went over a set of hurdles at practice, the upperclassmen gave me doubtful looks and whispered to one another in uncertain tones. But after I raced my first 60 meters, just an open 60 meters, one of the hurdlers said to me, "I didn't know that you were that good. We all thought you were just a little special, maybe on the spectrum, and we were questioning the coach why he would bring this athlete in to train with us."

We all laughed and joked about it, but then I realized it was due to me getting acclimated to a different level of competition. As I became more comfortable, I was able to jump those hurdles with ease and more confidence.

The race he was referring to was my first 60-meter race indoors at Clemson. It was the first time I'd gone against athletes who were bigger and more muscular than me, football players and track athletes. They were on their home turf, too, so the crowd cheered for them more than for us, the opponents.

I was so nervous when I got into my blocks because I didn't know what was going to happen. All I knew was that I had to stick to the plan.

As the starter said, "Set," we raised our hips. Then the gun went off, and I just ran as hard as I could. The only thing I could think of was the big cubic zirconia earrings I was wearing that were flapping against my jaw.

But I ran as hard as I could, as fast as I could, with the technique that I had been taught to come across the line. I ran a 6.62 and got the A standard. I didn't know anything about this. I had never run a 60 before, but this was a big deal, especially back then, as the A standard meant I had qualified for the NCAA Indoor Championships with my first race.

I came back to the dorms after our trip, and all my teammates were looking at me differently than they had before. At that moment, I realized that I could be a leader without using words. I could be a leader through example, sparking inspiration in my other teammates to go out there and be better athletes.

One athlete in particular took an interest in my new talent, and that was Leonard Scott. He was a junior when I was a freshman, and he was the guy on campus. Not only was he the fastest guy, but he also played football for the university. He was an amazing athlete, but also just a good character, fun, always laughing, just a good old country boy.

I had a private practice one day with Vince Anderson and Leonard Scott, and they wanted me to do some starts out of the blocks and run about 55 meters. I did that two or three times, and then they told me to stop and do it again. I think that's when they realized that they no longer had to look for a sprinter.

As the season went on, Leonard and I became that dynamic duo. I would go out and run a fast time, and then he would go out and run an even faster time. One time, at the University of Kentucky, we ran a 200 indoors. As I came across the finish line in my heat, the announcer said, "We have the world's fastest time right now in the 200-meter indoors, set by Justin Gatlin." Everyone was in shock and congratulated me, and I was happy.

The next heat came up, and Leonard Scott was in it. When the gun went off, he went out and bested my time. That was only about five minutes after my heat. That story repeated itself throughout my freshman year. I was in Leonard's shadow. I was the bridesmaid to his bride. I was riding shotgun, and he was driving.

When in a situation like that, where you're constantly getting bested, most people conform and realize that they aren't the best, but I knew that I could do better. I wanted to figure out how I could be better, not only better than Leonard but better than myself.

So, I started to study his technique. I started to train harder. And I used something that I knew would be a weakness for him: the time he had to spend on football. In the spring, while he was practicing with the football team, I was training for track. I used that time to build my speed and endurance, to get stronger, faster, and more confident.

By the time track season started, I had gotten better. It really showed at the NCAAs. I knew I had to prepare for them because not only was I going up against Leonard Scott, but I was also going against a guy named Ja'Warren Hooker. Hooker was a 19-second 200-meter runner that season, the only athlete in all of NCAA history at that time who had run sub-20. He was a Goliath, a monster, a dragon to be slain but also to be feared.

There was also Kim Collins, the indoor 60-meter world champion, 60-meter NCAA champion, and 200-meter indoor champion that year already. Outdoors, he seemed like a juggernaut, a guy who was not going to be beaten. He was backed by TCU, and he had teammates who were just as fast as him, and they could jump as well.

According to the stats, it looked like TCU was shooting for the NCAA trophy. They just had to seal the deal. But they didn't recognize how determined we were to be the best team out there.

As the season progressed, one of our javelin throwers had one of the best throws of the year, and we rallied around that. We used it as inspiration, and it sparked a fire within us.

We went to Oregon for the 2001 NCAAs, and I got ready for the 100-meter race. The prelims went very well. I won my heat. The semis also went well. Leonard Scott did great throughout his rounds. But between semis and finals, Leonard Scott suffered a hamstring injury and wasn't able to run the finals. It was on me to slay the dragons and bring home an NCAA championship.

As the gun went off for the 100-meter finals, I wondered how I was going to defeat the unbeatable Kim Collins and the plethora of other athletes who were ready for this moment as well.

Halfway through the race, I was not in the lead. Kim Collins was. But I kept striding, and with each step, I got closer and closer to Kim. When we got to the finish line, I had an epic lean for the finish and beat him. This shocked the world because everyone thought that Kim was going to win. He was on fire, but I took that victory. I took it because I wanted it more. I'd worked harder for it, and I knew that it was in my grasp. I wasn't going to let go.

My win in the 100 meters changed the whole dynamic of the championship. Now our team was going toe-to-toe, blow-for-blow, with TCU. TCU would win the long jump, but we would go and win a throw. TCU would come back and win the 4x100 against us, but then we would win the 200 meters.

I qualified for the 200 meters, and Leonard Scott was in that race, too. He came back. When I added up the points, all Kim Collins had to do was just finish that race. If he did, his team would win by one point.

We got in the blocks and into the set position. Then, before the gun went off, Kim Collins bolted from the blocks. False start. Clear, evident false start. When he stopped striding, the look on his face made it evident that he'd just made the biggest mistake of his life because now he was disqualified. Even if he'd have come in last place, his team would have won.

He gathered his bags and his clothes and moved them from the starting blocks, and then we got readjusted and reset. One monster was down, but that still left another, Ja'Warren Hooker, in the race.

When the gun went off, I ran for my life. I just remember hitting my top speed and holding it as long as I could, coming off that turn, burning the straightaway.

I gasped for air as I came across that finish line and looked up at the scoreboard. I'd broken the NCAA 200-meter record with a 19.86. The crowd went crazy. Not only did I come away with an NCAA record, but I also helped the University of Tennessee win our first championship in ten years.

We stood on top of that podium and sang "Rocky Top." We were so joyous. We were so happy. We knew that we were now a championship-caliber team, And that meant a lot to us. The trophy and the wins didn't really matter to me. It was the fight for them that meant something.

CHAPTER 7

# Forging a Champion: Part 2

Now it was time to reset myself for my sophomore year and make an even bigger splash. But something derailed me. As I got ready for the summer, my coach told me, "Let's go try to make a Junior World team." That was sanctioned by USA Track & Field, not the NCAA. To get on the team, you had to declare all the medications and supplements you were taking.

Now, I had been diagnosed with ADD in the second grade. My diagnosis at that early age stemmed from clear signs that my teacher noticed. One day, we were taking a standardized test, and a bird flew next to the window and started chirping. All of the kids in my class were distracted by this bird, but when they refocused on the test, I didn't. I remember thinking, *Where is this bird from? What kind of bird is it? Where's its home? Does it have babies? What kind of food does it eat?* All these things were running through my mind when I should have been focused on taking this test.

That was clear evidence for my teacher to tell my parents, "I think you need to take Justin to get tested to see if he has ADD or ADHD." They did, and ADD was the diagnosis. I started taking Zoloft and Adderall to try to find the right combination.

One of the symptoms of taking this medication is a lack of hunger. At that age, I felt that taking medication meant that you were sick. And if it was for your brain, it meant that you were slow. So, I was very embarrassed about taking the medication. I had to leave the classroom every day throughout elementary school, middle school, and high school to take my medication every day in the nurse's office. It made me feel less than, so I usually hid it from others.

Before I went to college, we told the coaches and the school that I had a learning disability and was taking medication. My freshman year, it wasn't a problem. I was taking my medication, and that's okay with NCAA rules because you are a student before you're an athlete. I took multiple drug tests, and they never came back positive.

But for this USA-sanctioned event, my coach, who filled out the form for me, did not declare the medication that I took. He didn't check a box. That's what it was—he just didn't check that one box. So, I went out there and competed, and I made history, qualifying for the World Junior team.

But then, a month after qualifying, my parents got a letter in the mail saying that I had tested positive for a banned substance and wouldn't be able to be a part of this USA team. I was beside myself. *Positive? What could I possibly have tested positive for?*

I only took my Adderall medication. All my other supplements were natural. When we went through the findings, we discovered that the test had detected minute traces of amphetamines. At that age, I didn't even know what amphetamines were. I don't think my parents knew, either, but we still didn't correlate it with my ADD medication because we never thought about the chemical makeup of the medication from second grade on.

I was heartbroken because I felt as though something that had always embarrassed me had now derailed me in the one thing I was most passionate about. In my view, Adderall never gave me an advantage. If anything, it put me at a disadvantage because it made me focus, made me dial in, and with certain workouts, that's something you don't want to do.

If you're running 300-meter repeats, you don't want to focus too much. You want to go into a zone and just kind of run through the practice because when you focus, you focus on every step, you focus on every breath, and you focus on how fast your heart rate is going. That is something you really don't want as an elite runner.

My parents and I got through the setback. We didn't fight against it because it was true. I did take Adderall. I took the blame for that. It didn't disqualify me from running in NCAA meets, but I was banned for two years from participating in USA-sanctioned meets.

So, I just stuck to college and ran my NCAA campaign in 2002, my sophomore year, tapping back into that championship mentality. I didn't let this adversity get in my way. Instead, I used that fire inside of me to prove to people who were calling me a drug cheat, to prove to people who were doubting my true talent, that I was genuinely a runner with God-given talent who could run with the best of them.

In my sophomore year, I won the 60-meter indoor and 200-meter indoor NCAA titles, and I won the SEC titles for both as well. We also won the indoor team NCAA title, which had never been done by the University of Tennessee before.

Then we went on to the outdoor season, where I had an amazing run at the SEC Championship, winning the 100 meters. I backed it up and broke the NCAA record again in the 200 meters at Mississippi State, and I also threatened to win the 110 hurdles, nearly besting the guy who was the defending NCAA champion. So, undoubtedly, this was one of the best track meets I'd had.

To defend our NCAA title, we had to race at LSU. We'd beaten TCU the year before, and this time, LSU rose to the occasion. They had amazing athletes on their team. But we were ready. We had our dynamic duo of Leonard Scott and Justin Gatlin, and we had added a few athletes from around the world to our team. That NCAA Championship played out like a story.

We battled for the next four days, event by event. LSU won a lot of them, we won a lot of them, and it came down to the relay. During the relay, we came around to make the last exchange, and LSU ran out of the zone. The crowd could see it, but it was on the referees to flag it as a disqualification.

Mind you, LSU was on their home turf. No referee flagged them, and they went on to win the NCAA title by seven points. If they'd been disqualified, we would have won the title. We would have been the consecutive team, winning two NCAA championships back to back. It was a heartbreaking moment for us because we had worked very hard that season to win, and it felt like it had been ripped away from us.

As I finished that campaign, we're still having a very successful season. I got another letter in the mail from the USADA, which is the USA Anti-Doping Agency. They had dealt with me for two years, as I was not able to run any USA Track & Field-sanctioned events. The letter stated that they had reduced my two years to one year with time served. So, my sophomore year was the only year I had to sit out.

I truly believe that because of the cessation that I was showing throughout my sophomore campaign, they knew that there was nothing else I could do in college. They let me go out there and become a pro, which is what I did.

But before that happened, I had to sit down with Vince Anderson and tell him exactly what I was thinking. I sat in his office and said, "Coach, I've done all I can do in college. I think it's time for me to look for different goals to set, different competition."

He looked at me and said, "I believe that you're a hundred percent right, Justin. There's nothing left for you at this level."

"If I turn pro," I said, "I still want to be here. I still want to be coached by you."

He paused for a second and then said, "Justin, we've always been real with each other. And I'll be honest with you. I want you to stay here. I want you to be coached by me. But I want you to also realize the totem pole of the things I have to be able to do in my life. First is my family. I have to make sure my family's good. Second, are these kids on this University of Tennessee track team. And then third, third would be you. As a professional athlete, you have to come third to everything else that is my life, my love, and my job."

Hearing him say it that way didn't make me mad or upset because he had always been honest with me, and I appreciated that about him. But I told him, "I think that I am going to turn pro."

In my rookie year, I needed someone who could focus on me to make sure that I was doing things properly and not making a lot of mistakes. So, I decided to part ways with Coach Anderson and the University of Tennessee and turn pro.

Now that you have laid out a passion-driven goal, it is time to level up. Take the word "goal" out of the equation and replace it with "mission." You are probably asking why. While goals are important, they are taken for granted or delayed for other pressing matters. A mission comes off with a sense of urgency and accountability. I have learned that the classic question, "Where do you see yourself in 5-10 years?" is like a shot in the dark. Your life can change drastically in a decade or a half decade. I have watched Olympic champions achieve their goal and not be able to defend their title just four years later. You do not know what obstacles lie five to ten years ahead. But with a one to two-year plan, you can realistically map out a plan for success. Be passionate about knowing your mission inside and out. Know all the details and study all the variables. Do not become a victim of circumstance. Face the fears of the future and own your destiny.

To help you take further steps to become your best self, follow the action steps I have listed below.

- Give yourself a 1-2 year plan to achieve your mission.
- Breakdown how you could win:
    o Assess your time management and design it for ultimate success.
    o Study your competition and their strategy, and analyze the data.
    o Know beyond a shadow of a doubt that you will win, and establish consistency in that feeling through tradition in daily action that you commit to every step of the way.

- Breakdown how you could lose, as well:
    o Losing is not understanding your variables.
    o Examine how different situations could derail your success.
    o Create a strategy that addresses those different variables and attack it with purpose.

# CHAPTER 8

# My Mount Everest: Part 1

I struggled with the idea of going pro. I hadn't officially declared that I was because once you do, you are renouncing competing at the college level. With my parents' guidance, I said, "Hey, let's take a break this summer and figure out exactly what going pro will look like." So, we went on a road trip to visit some family in New York City.

While there, I got a phone call from a number that I didn't recognize at all. I answered, and someone said, "Hey, is this Justin Gatlin?" The person had a heavy Jamaican accent.

"Yeah, this is Justin," I said cautiously.

"Hey, this is Trevor Graham."

I paused and then said, "Okay, Trevor, nice to meet you."

"You don't know who I am?" he asked in a tone that implied that I should know.

"No," I said. "I don't know who you are."

He chuckled. "I'm Marion Jones and Tim Montgomery's coach."

At that point in time, Marion Jones was a household name. Everyone knew who she was. She was like the modern-day Flo-Jo. Everyone was excited to be around Marion and to watch her run. She was the show. And he was her coach.

I got a little giddy. My parents were listening in on the conversation, as I had the speakerphone on. Trevor said, "I'm reaching out to you on behalf of myself and Nike. We want to see if you want to sign with us and work with us moving forward." I was still in college at the time, so Nike couldn't talk to me directly.

Trevor couldn't see me, but my eyes were really big. I was thinking, *Man, I'm getting scouted by Nike, the people who make the best sprint shoes, the people who make Air Jordans. This is a company that has built its name with champions, and the people there recognize my pedigree.* Not only could I sign with a great company, but I could also be working with one of the best coaches in the profession. That was an exciting moment for me.

At that point, my mom pumped the brakes on the conversation, saying, "We appreciate you reaching out, but we are handling family business right now. We'll reach out to you when we're done with our vacation."

After I hung up, I was still beside myself. *This is amazing*, I thought. *I didn't know that I was even on their radar.*

When I got back to college for the 2003 fall semester, my mind was in a rush. I was focused on what the future had in store for me and not so much on college.

I slowly started to tell some of my close friends and teammates that I was seriously considering going pro. Whispers spread throughout the team and campus. Eventually, the AD came to me and said, "Come see me in my office. Let's talk." Obviously, the whispers had gotten to him, and he knew exactly what was going on. When I met with him, he asked me what I was thinking of doing. I said, "I'm leaning towards going pro."

"Give us another year," he said. We're going to make sure that you get a deal with Adidas." At that time, Tennessee was sponsored by Adidas. "We're going to make sure that you have the best deal possible."

"But how can you guarantee that?" I asked him. "What if I get hurt my junior year? What does that look like for me?"

He really had no rebuttal. He just kept saying, "Give us one more year. Give us one more year."

I told him I'd think about it and then left. In the meantime, I did research. I've forgotten how the information came to me, but in my two years at the University of Tennessee, they made ten million dollars from our team championships. We were very successful. I connected the dots and realized it wasn't just about the winning; it was also about the income that was coming in with the winning. There were no NIL deals then, no way for a college athlete like myself to make any money or earn my just due financially from all of my hard work. This pushed me even more to go pro.

Finally, I decided to do it. I sat with my parents, and we declared that I was going to go pro. We had another conversation with Trevor, and then we had a conversation with Tim Phelan, my future Nike rep. But we were missing one component, which was an agent. During my sophomore year, at Nationals, I was getting vetted by different agents.

I met with the legendary Renaldo Nehemiah for lunch with my family, and we talked about what going pro would mean. He nonchalantly said, "If you get an opportunity, just give me a call and tell me what you think." So, he was one of the guys at the top of our list for representation. There was also a snowball effect, with one person referring me to another, and so on. So, Nike referred me to Trevor Graham, and then Trevor Graham referred me to Charlie Wells, who was Marion Jones and Tim Montgomery's agent.

To make everything flow and be more cohesive, I was told, "You want to sign with Nike. You'll love what they have for you and what they offer. He's a Nike coach. He's also working with these athletes." It made sense to me and my family to keep it all a one-stop shop, so I signed with Charlie Wells and his team. I was very excited about that because now I had the coach, I had the agent, and I was about to sign this historic deal with Nike.

Mr. John Capriotti himself, who was running the track and field division worldwide for Nike, came to Pensacola, sat at our dinner table, and gave us the contract. I looked it over with my new agency rep, Lou Emma Starks, and we gave it a thumbs up. We were good to go.

Before we signed, I remember having a conversation with my mom about the negotiation process. We didn't know much about Nike contracts or even track and field professional contracts at all.

There was another athlete who had been out there making waves at an early age in high school, and he was going to leave after his freshman year with Michigan to go pro, and that was Alan Webb. Alan Webb was the first high school athlete to break the sub-four minute barrier in the mile, so he was already a rock star. People were following him, and he was also looking to sign with Nike. We just made it really simple. We said, "Allen is doing amazing things, and we know we've been doing amazing things. So, we don't want to get paid any less than what he's getting paid, and we would like more, if possible." The contract was basically constructed in that manner. Going forward, I think we were all pleased.

We signed the contract, and now I was officially a Nike athlete. Going into my 2003 indoor campaign with Nike, I was able to wear my first professional suit. I was excited; I'd made it. As we started training, Nike also showed me a lot of love. "We're going to make a shoe just for you," they said. "This is going to be the shoe that all the athletes you ran with in the past and the young athletes who are coming behind you are going to want." It was my own track spikes, and it was called the G5. I helped construct the shoe, and it really was me.

Now I was a professional athlete with my own pair of track spikes that athletes from anywhere around the world could buy. It was in *East Bay Magazine*, which was a popular place to buy track and field equipment during that era. It was such an amazing feeling.

During my first couple of days of practice as a professional athlete, I got my ass kicked. Some guys were much stronger. I was still 18 years old, and I was running against grown men. I was also the golden boy, the new guy on the block, so I was a target for a lot of these hungry professionals who weren't getting paid as much as me, and they weren't getting as much attention as me, either.

At times, I'd be in the starting blocks or running reps at practice, and I could tell their competitive level was so much higher because it was personal but not personal. They wanted to make a point: "You've got to earn your spot. They may have given you this chance because of what you've done in college, but now you have to earn your spot." I respected that.

I worked hard, and I studied a lot. Trevor Graham made a living in North Carolina, where I had to move to train, which was very home-like for me. I was away from my parents and college teammates, and it was a foreign environment. I was living on my own, though I was barely 20 years old. I know it probably drove my parents crazy that I wasn't at an institute where I could be held accountable, where I had to keep up my grades or be in class on time, somewhere with real structure. I was out in the world now. I had to practice in the morning, but the rest of my day was for me. So, Trevor Graham reassured my parents, telling them that I was going to be taken care of and not to worry. I think that put them at ease.

As I finished training and started to gain the respect of my teammates, I was gearing up, getting ready, getting faster, and getting stronger for my first indoor professional race, which was at Madison Square Garden. Two people really stuck out to me in that 60-meter indoor race: my idol, the legendary Maurice Greene, who was still a relevant and very dominant athlete, and Terrence Trammell, whom I'd seen compete in college. Terrence was a couple of years older than me and ran for the University of South Carolina. He was truly a talented athlete; he was a sprinter and hurdler like myself, so he was someone I definitely looked up to. And I knew that he was capable of being successful in both events.

Terrence Trammell was on a roll that year, and he wasn't too keen on Maurice Greene. Anytime he was in a race, he was determined to beat Maurice's crew. I happened to be in one of those races, my first race in Madison Square Garden, and I wanted to make sure that I gave it my all. Team Nike, John Capriotti himself, my agency, my parents, they were all sitting in the stands to watch my first race.

As we lined up for the race, the guy in lane eight was obviously upset—and he had a right to be. Water was dripping from the ceiling into his lane. He threw his hands up two or three times at the starting line and complained about the water. That was Shawn Crawford, and I knew that he was a formidable opponent as well. But I was focused on Terrence Trammell and Maurice Greene.

Finally, we got in the blocks, the gun went off, and I ran through my phases. Coming out of my drive phase, I started to accelerate and gain momentum, and I caught up with Maurice Greene. Terrence Trammell came in first, I came in second, and Maurice Greene came in third. In my first professional race, I'd beaten my idol, a legend, the world record holder in the 60 meters and the 100 meters.

I remember looking up into the stands and seeing the pride on my Nike teammates' faces, on my agent's face and on my parents' faces. We were off to a great start.

In the next race, I ran even faster, finishing the 60 meters in 6.45 seconds. That was one of the fastest times, if not the fastest time, in the world. Now I was ready for the Indoor World Championships in Birmingham, England.

My two biggest opponents at that time were Mark Lewis Francis and Jason Gardner, the speedsters for Team Great Britain. As for America, only two sprinters could qualify for the 60-meter indoors, and Terrence Trammell was first while I was second. As we were training for the race in the UK, Terrence suffered a hamstring injury, so he wasn't able to compete that year. That meant it was all on me again, almost like déjà vu with Leonard Scott and my 2001 campaign to win the 100 meters against Kim Collins. Now it was happening again with Team USA.

I went through the rounds, winning all the prelims. Then, in the finals, when the gun went off, I made sure that I was ahead of the pack, ahead of those two athletes, and I came across the finish line victorious. That was my first gold medal as a professional athlete and the first time I was a world champion in an event. I was so elated; to say I was happy would be an understatement. So far, I had succeeded in every challenge that I'd faced.

After winning the indoor championships, I turned my sights to the outdoor track season, and I soon found success there as well. My first outdoor race was in Mexico City, which is at a very high altitude. Well, they tell you that you're going to run faster at high altitudes, but they don't tell you that you have to drink more water because you're going to get dehydrated more quickly.

As I warmed up for the 200-meter race, I thought, *This is my opportunity. I can run even faster than I did in college. I can run 19.7. I'm going to do something amazing at this track meet.* But at the same time, I was becoming more and more tired. *Why am I so tired after warming up?* I wondered. No one told me that I should have been drinking more water.

Finally, the race began, and as I rounded the bend and went into the straightaway, I pulled my hamstring. I'd never felt pain like that before. It was the first time I'd had an injury serious enough to sideline me. I limped over to the infield and lay there in disbelief. It felt like I had been shot.

Two medics came over with an old-school stretcher, the kind you have to pick up and carry. No wheels, no nothing, just a mat with two rods on each side. They put me on the stretcher and carried me across the field. I was so embarrassed because I couldn't walk. All I could do was lay there on the stretcher.

It took me some time to heal, and I came back earlier than I should have. The injury wasn't quite gone yet. Because of this, when I competed at the Outdoor Nationals, I re-injured my hamstring in the first round of the 100 meters.

I still remember what people whispered about me: "See, I told you he wasn't really made of anything. He's a fluke. He's not going to do anything at the professional level." What hurt the most about this was that I couldn't do anything about it because I was injured.

Michael Johnson came up to me afterward and said, "One thing that I learned about being a professional athlete is that if you're hurt, don't run. Don't try to go out there and be bigger and better than anybody else. It's about being healthy. That's the only way you're going to be successful in this space." I took that to heart.

Another conversation I had before leaving Nationals was with the relay coach. Each team is assigned a relay coach. Ours was the coach at the University of Texas. "I know that I didn't make the team," I said to him, "but am I still able to qualify for the relay pool?"

"I know you have it in you," he replied. "If you heal up, go out and run, and show that you can run the fastest time in the world this year, I'll make sure you're on that relay. I'll make sure you're part of this team."

That gave me real hope. I went back home, and there I trained, healed up, and got better and faster.

In the months leading up to the World Championships, I raced in Berlin and lost badly. I felt fatigued, and I came in fifth. I'd never got fifth place in a race in my life. I didn't understand what had happened. Back at the hotel, I sat in the tub with the shower running over me, feeling down on myself. I realized that the ratio of success to failure in track and field is imbalanced. You're going to lose more than you're going to win, but you have to control how you're going to win and when you're going to win.

My next race was in Zurich, Switzerland, maybe less than a week later. When I stood at the starting line, I felt on the threshold of an epic moment because it was raining hard. As the rain came down, I got in the blocks, and when the gun went off, all the rage and frustration inside me boiled up. I took it all out on that race. At the finish line, it was a three-way tie between me, Kim Collins, and John Capel, and we'd all set the world's fastest time. It was the first time I'd ever gone sub 10. Now I was a part of the sub-10 club. I was happy, particularly because I'd reached the requirement that Coach Bubba had set for me to be a part of the USA relay team.

I went through the whole process, signing up to be a part of the team, and I was thrilled because now it felt real. The campaign in 2003 was in Paris, France, and when I joined the team for the trip, the other athletes looked at me kind of funny, like they were thinking, *Why are you here again?*

When I met the coaches at the venue, they said, "Check in at the tent and get your credentials." But when I got to the front of the line at the check-in tent, my name wasn't on the list. I wasn't even in the database. They were like, "We don't even know who you are or why you're here."

As you can imagine, this made me kind of frantic. One of the things that really scared me was being lost in Europe, in a whole different world where people didn't speak the same language as me.

I called my agent. Due to the time difference, he was still asleep in America, but he woke up and answered. "What's going on?" he asked in a groggy voice.

"I'm stuck here," I told him. "I'm not qualified. They didn't give me my credentials. What should I do?"

He paused for a second, and I said, "Hello? Hello?"

Finally, he said, "What do you want me to do about it?" and he hung up. I was stuck in Europe. My worst fear had come true.

I stood there, confused about what to do. The rest of Team USA had gotten their credentials and gone past the checkpoint. They were now inside the athlete village, while I was stuck outside by myself.

The CEO of USA Track & Field, Craig Masback, rolled up. He walked up to me and said, "What's going on?" I told him my situation, and he helped me get into the village. But now I felt alienated because Coach Bubba hadn't lived up to his word. I wasn't a part of this team. The only thing I could do was sit and watch Team USA from the stands as they competed and won championships.

Looking down at the stadium track, I said to myself, *I will never sit in the stands ever again and watch a track meet unless I want to.* That was the motivation I got from the 2003 World Championships in Paris to catapult me into 2004.

But I still had one race left in my 2003 season. In between the Paris championships and this last race in Russia, my parents and I had it out with Charlie Wells and told him that at the end of the season, we were going to part ways.

The meet in Russia was a monumental event. There had never been anything like it before. It was a race for a million dollars. Yes, the prize for winning the 100 meters was a million dollars. A million dollars for running just 9 or 10 seconds. But you had to win.

It was around 45 degrees in Russia at that time. I also thought that, as I was American, everyone would look at me differently due to our two countries' history. They had always been our enemy in some way, and I wondered if this was something that I would have to fear. Turns out, it wasn't.

Some people were very nice, very helpful, very obliging—but the food, though, wasn't amazing at all. I found myself going to McDonald's almost every day while I was there. I was homesick. I don't think I've ever told my parents this, but I was on the hotel room phone constantly, talking to my girlfriend back in America. I think I left that hotel with a $2,000 bill just from using the phone. Welcome to the professional world and welcome to the world of travel. It was a crazy reminder that I couldn't always do things when I wanted to do them.

Just before the race was about to start, the starter said, "Take your sweats off, put your running gear on, and stand behind your blocks." We all looked at each other as if to say, "Man, I'm not taking my sweats off. It is freezing out here." But we all reluctantly did.

The starter fired the gun, and I ran as hard as I could. I was running for a million dollars. And when I crossed that finish line, I was first, with a time of 10.05, I believe.

The first person to congratulate me was Charlie Wells. He jumped out of the stands wearing a long trench coat that made him look like some kind of superhero, like Batman coming to the rescue. His job as my agent was to collect my winnings and take his percentage, so he was thrilled at the outcome.

But my encounter with him was lackluster. He was very excited about being paid. He went to the meet promoters and requested to be paid only his percentage of my earnings, deviating from the usual practice where he would collect all the money, take his cut, and then give me my share. In truth, he took more than his share and simply left my portion of the winnings on the table, leaving it up to me to collect it on my own. Then, he parted ways with me, leaving me without any money or an agent.

Having this huge check for a million dollars but without a cent to my name, the only person my parents and I knew to call was Renaldo Nehemiah, the agent who had vetted us just a year ago. We were so gracious that Renaldo was going to take us on even though we had decided not to work with him previously.

Renaldo worked on getting that money. He negotiated with the meet promoters in Russia, who had put on an amazing show. They'd even given us cloaks and crowns to wear, and the winners got to ride in horse-drawn chariots around the track and wave to the crowd.

But, of course, my horse was the rebel. It almost got loose, and I thought I was going to have to jump off the back of this chariot and tuck and roll onto the ground. Thankfully, it didn't come to that. The horse eventually calmed down, and the show went on.

Renaldo did everything he could, and a company called Octagon assisted him. I was very happy with the decision to use him because, ultimately, he was successful. I knew, from that moment on, that we would be working together throughout my whole career.

CHAPTER 9

# My Mount Everest: Part 2

As we went into the 2004 campaign, Trevor said to me, "We had a good season last year, but we need to turn it up now. We need to be more competitive in 2004. I'm going to bring in another athlete who's going to push you to be better, stronger, and more competitive. May the best man win."

One day, I was in the gym, and in walked Shawn Crawford. Shawn was a beast of a man, with a huge upper body, slim waist, and short, powerful legs. The first time I saw him really train in the gym, he did ten reps of 225 pounds on the incline bench with no spotter. I said to myself, "This guy is going to be a problem."

When I spoke to my dad about Shawn, he agreed: "Yeah, man. I thought Leonard was going to be a problem for you, but this guy is going to be even tougher to beat."

But I stayed within myself and said, "Let's focus on what we're here for, to be the best." When you have good athletes around you, not only do you see how good they are, but you also see their weaknesses. So, I used the same strategy with Shawn that I used with Leonard. As I started to train with him, I realized that there were certain things that I could do better than him and certain things that he did better than me, and I tried to use that to make myself a more complete athlete.

That year, I had to race against Maurice Greene again. This time, though, it wasn't 60 meters; it was 100 meters, the race he was known for. The race was in Palo Alto, California.

The race began, and when I came out of my drive phase, I found myself running stride for stride with Maurice Greene. For whatever reason, it was a different feeling than the 60 meters. I was starstruck—in awe. I was like, *I'm racing my idol in the 100 meters.* It was like a "come-to-Jesus" moment, in a way, so surreal.

While I was having these emotions and thoughts, he pulled away from me and crossed the finish line with a new world record. It was wild, and I was still in disbelief. But my agent and coach brought me back to reality. "Don't let that happen again. You're here to do a job, not to be a fanboy." From that moment on, I vowed to respect my competitors, no matter who they were, but otherwise, we were at war. That was what we were there for—to compete at the highest level.

Later in the 2004 season, in walked a new rival that I wasn't prepared for: Asafa Powell. I'd never even known he existed. He was a young Jamaican sprint star who'd just come onto the scene, and he was dominating. He was a complete sprinter. It was hard to detect whether he was going to be weak or strong; he had a solid race. Powell had a great start, great transition, great acceleration, and he just dominated. He was beating Maurice Greene everywhere around the world, and I was third or fourth most of the time that season. I didn't win any 100-meter races that year. As we got closer to the 2004 Olympic trials, I was projected to win them. But I didn't win. Maurice Greene beat me, although I still made the Olympic team.

With the pressure of being on the front of track and field news and hearing my doubters and other opponents in the war yelling, "We're going to take you down! We're going to beat you!" The mental warfare was at a whole different level.

But we were successful. My training partner, Shawn Crawford, and I decided that while we might not be the same athlete or have the same interests, we had to think of ourselves as detectives working together to go out and fight this crime. And we made a pact: "If you're first, I'm second. If you're seventh, I'm eighth," and so on. We weren't going to let anybody split us up because we knew how hard we had worked to get to this point.

Shawn and I both qualified for the 100 and 200 for the 2004 Olympic team, and we were very excited about it. When we got to the

Olympic Village in Athens, Greece, where the games had started, it felt like we were part of something special. This wasn't just any Olympics. The Olympic torch had finally come home, and we were a part of that moment.

Shawn and I made it through the first round, which was at eight in the morning. In the semis, we were in the same heat. The race started, and when we reached the 70-meter mark, we were right next to each other in the lanes, in full stride. Shawn looked over at me and said, "Are you ready to get to this final?"

"You're damn right I am," I replied, and then we crossed the finish line together. We were so pumped up. We thought that was the coolest thing in the world because we were performing our craft at a high level, and we still were able to talk to each other and communicate. The commentators thought differently. They thought it was tacky and distasteful. But it was one of those experiences where we were just being us. We were being true to what we felt, and we stuck to our guns.

The finals were electrifying. We came out 15 minutes before our race was even ready to start. They started playing Greek music in the stadium, and people were chanting and clapping together. It felt like the heavyweight bout of the world was about to go off, and everyone had been waiting for this moment.

All the athletes warmed up on the competition track, which is unheard of. As we got behind our blocks, I had a conversation with God, saying, "This is the moment that I've been waiting for ever since I knew that track and field was a thing. I want to become the Olympic champion. If I win this race, thank you. I am humbly, humbly thankful for this moment. And if I don't, I will go back to the drawing board and work harder."

As the race unfolded, I ran harder than I have ever run in my life. But when I came across the finish line, I had won with a time of 9.85 seconds. Second place was 9.86 seconds. Third place was 9.87 seconds. Fourth place was 9.88 seconds. That's how slim the margins were between gold, silver, bronze, and not even being on the podium. It was an epic race, but I'd come in first.

Francis Obikwelu got second, Maurice Greene got third, Shawn Crawford got fourth, and Asafa Powell got fifth. The crowd was going crazy, and I remember watching the video and an announcer saying, "We thought he could do it, but we never thought he would ever do it. We knew he was able to do it, but we didn't think he was going to do it." With the wreath on my head, I found my parents in the stands and hugged them. I'd done it. I was an Olympic champion, and I was still only in the sophomore year of my professional career. It was such a magical moment—one I'll never forget.

When I came back home to Pensacola, I was greeted like a king. We had a signing at the civic center, a huge place, and it was sold out. The whole city came out to see me, get autographs, and take pictures with me, and I stood in that line signing autographs for two hours straight. The line was wrapped around the building. With me were other legends of our city, like Roy Jones, Jr., and Derrick Brooks. It was an amazing experience. There was even a billboard with a picture of me coming across the finish line, and the title said, "Just in time, the Olympic gold champion."

The love I felt from the community fired me up for the 2005 season. I was a champion, so I had to operate as a champion. I had a great team around me, but I was missing just one element for it to be a championship team; a therapist. I decided to work with Chris Webstein, who was a Nike-paid therapist. It made sense because not only was he a great therapist, Nike was footing the bill for his services. He understood biomechanics, tissue, and how to stretch properly, but he also knew how to give a great massage. He was a Renaissance man, a one-stop shop, an army of one when it came to therapeutic recovery.

The only thing I worried about was sealing the deal by becoming a champion again. The Outdoor World Championships were in Helsinki, Finland, and I was ready to run. I had qualified for both the 100 and 200. I came across the line victorious in the 100 meters.

The box that was still unchecked was winning the 200. I'd run the 200 prelims the day before, and the night before, I'd won the 100-meter finals, so I had no time to rest. The sprinters I had to race against in the 200 meters were fresh and ready to run. But then a storm came in, delaying the race for a day. I knew this was my moment, that God was telling me, "If you can make something from this day, so be it. Become a champion. Show the world that you're a champion."

Two or three other sprinters had run faster than me that season in the 200 meters. They had been tearing up the track all season long. But when the race started, I got out in front. As I came across that turn, I didn't let anybody pass me. I fought tooth and nail to cross that finish line first, and I came out victorious. It was the first time Team USA swept all the way down to fourth place. I got first, Wallace Spearman got second, John Capel got third, and Tyson Gay got fourth. It was monumental.

That moment showed me that I wasn't a fluke. It showed the world I wasn't a fluke. I was a bona fide champion. The win gave me opportunities outside of track and field. I was a part of the Thanksgiving Day Parade in New York City, on one of the floats with the singer

Fantasia. I even scored big deals with Wheaties. And we all know that being on a Wheaties box means you are a true champion. Michael Jordan, Michael Phelps, Serena Williams, Jerry Rice, Tom Brady—dominating athletes, real champions—have all graced the front of a Wheaties box, and now I had as well. I also scored big deals with Canon, Hershey's, and Power Bar, which eclipsed what I was also doing with Nike.

It is such a deflating feeling when you have worked so hard and accomplished all your team goals, but greed still rears its ugly head. After winning the double gold in 2005, I believe Chris felt like he should have been compensated more even though Nike was already paying him handsomely. It was a confusing time for me because I was still young. I was still in my early 20s and didn't understand how to properly conduct business. I just remember being told unanimously by my parents, coach and agent, "If he's not going to handle business and you feel like he is robbing you, trying to get paid double, fire him or let him leave." And that's what happened. We parted ways.

I always look at the positive side of things, so I thought, *Maybe we can look past our disagreement and still work together*. I also thought that with such short notice going into the 2006 season, it would be impossible to replace him.

I rehired Chris, and I still remember my mom saying these exact words: "You never hire somebody you've fired, especially if you fired them in a way that makes them disgruntled. They're never going to operate the same or be the same individual you once thought they were." She was right.

Going into 2006, there was only one thing left for me to do: break the 100-meter world record, 9.77 seconds, currently held by Asafa Powell. But I was ready for the challenge. In grand fashion, in my first race, I set a new world record: 9.76 seconds.

But then something happened. A few days later, they rolled my time back to 9.77. I don't know why. Maybe there was something wrong with the timing system, or maybe they just wanted to see something that had never been seen before: two people co-owning the world record in the 100 meters. This was setting up to be an amazing season because now there were two people ready to duke it out for the world record in the same era.

To top off all of my accolades, I won an Espy in 2006, the first awarded to a track athlete. It's one of my most prized possessions, and winning it was an amazing experience.

Uphill battles bring the sweetest victories. Let your path to success be your blueprint for life in general. Success is universally built off of *hard work, determination, dedication,* and *passion.* You know what lies ahead. No one rolls out of bed and says, "I think I'm going to climb a mountain today!" You have to be prepared for the task at hand. You need to be equipped with the necessary tools and knowledge. There will be sacrifices made along the way. Life and your mission are this mountain that towers in front of you. Do not be afraid to climb that mountain to your success. If you do not climb it to achieve your goal, someone else will.

---

Take action today by following the steps below.

- Be your biggest critic and fan.
- Critique yourself:
    - Analyze and objectively study your performance data.
    - Give yourself constructive criticism that helps you identify areas of weakness that could compromise your success.
    - Do not fear your imperfections; they are an opportunity to empower your choices to elevate your performance.

- Inspire yourself:
    - Embody the pinnacle of your success before you even get there.
    - Write down the daily steps you would take at the apex of your career.
    - Rehearse them regularly to help you ingrain them into your very being.

- From the way you wake up, get dressed, work out, and execute your daily actions, BE that person.
- Stay motivated by remembering where you have been so it can illuminate the path of where you are going.

CHAPTER 10

# Purgatory: Part 1

In three short years, I had accomplished more than most athletes do in their entire careers—winning Olympic gold in 2004, becoming a double World Champion in 2005, and setting a world record in 2006. I felt so honored. I felt like a real champion. The sky was the limit for me. I was the next legendary sprinter, and I was so happy about this.

I had a friend, Tim, who worked for USA Track & Field who was setting up his own Kansas City relays. At these relays, it was just about having a good time. College athletes could watch professional athletes run and see what it was like to compete at that level. This was needed, especially in that part of America. There were no Midwest relays. Everything was in Florida and Texas or at Mt. SAC. Those were the popular relays.

Tim came to me and said, "I would love for you to come out here and run a relay for the grand opening of my Kansas City relays." I was honored. He was such a good friend, always inspiring me to be a champion and stay humble. So, I decided to go. I wasn't even running for money; I did it because it was a great opportunity to stretch my legs and compete.

On top of that, I would get to race Maurice Greene in the 100 meters or the 60 meters, and we would go head to head in a relay, as we were both the fourth legs for our teams. He was Team HSI, and I was Team Sprint Capital.

As the relays approached, the stands were packed. People were so excited to be able to watch this because it had never really happened before. We were making history.

The gun went off, and the race began. The first leg handed the baton off to the second leg, the second leg handed the baton off to the third leg, and the teams were almost neck and neck. But once I got the stick, it was all over. I never looked back. We were victorious. We won the relay. It was a happy moment! However, the series of events after the win was a bit abnormal.

Usually, when you're done running, you go back to the warm-up area, or you go to a press conference. The press conference lasts about ten minutes, depending on how tough the competition was and where you placed. Then you go back to the warm-up area, do your cool-down, and get a massage. This helps flush all of the lactic acid out of your body so you can bounce back and get ready for your next competition.

Since I only ran one race that day, after the relay, I was done for the day. But then I started doing interviews before I got to the press conference, and Chris Webstein came over and started rubbing my legs. I thought, *Why is he so eager to work on me? We're done for the day.* But I didn't think anything more of it. Maybe he felt like he needed to find his place and show his worth to get paid more.

When he finished rubbing me down, I noticed he had gloves on. It still didn't dawn on me that anything was wrong. I felt like the people around me were my friends, and that included the people I worked with. When I was successful, they were successful. When I ate, they ate.

As I got ready for the press conference, my legs started tingling, which was unusual. But at the same time, I thought maybe it was Icy Hot or some anti-inflammatory to help my legs bounce back. After the relays were over, we celebrated and had a great night. I was on a high. I was the man in track and field, and I was becoming a household name. When I won in Kansas City, a few things felt out of sequence. It's only with 20/20 hindsight that I was able to look back and realize what had happened.

CHAPTER 11

# Purgatory: Part 2

Everything came crashing down a couple of months later when a letter arrived at my parents' home. After reading it, they immediately called my agent and discussed it with him. Then my agent gave me a call.

I can still hear the words that came out of my agent's mouth about testing positive. I instantly began to grieve, and I kept saying over and over, "I'm done. I'm done. I'm finished. I'm done." I already knew what I was up against after testing positive back in college. Two strikes and you're out. That's what this sport is all about. If you test positive once, and then, two years later, you test positive again, that's a lifetime ban. There was no way around it. At least, that's what I felt at that moment. Then I pulled myself together emotionally. It was time to figure out how to get around this.

At the same time, the situation with BALCO hit the news. A lot of big names were coming out in the scandal: Marion Jones, Barry Bonds, and Tim Montgomery. It was just bad timing. With all of this happening, my parents told me to just come home.

I was being attacked by the media and being dragged through the mud on social media. Everyone was taking shots at me. I didn't know which way to turn. So, I packed my bags to go back to Pensacola. This wasn't just a vacation. I sold my house within a month and moved back in with my parents.

Living with them made me feel really defeated. I had worked hard to be independent, to live out in the world, to show that I was a man, that I could take care of myself and be successful in doing so. And now, I found myself confined to a bedroom as a grownup while still trying to operate as a grownup.

As we prepared for these court proceedings, I found myself drinking and partying every day with friends I'd made in Pensacola as an adult. It was a very rough time for me, but I had to pull myself together. It was hard, and it didn't instantly happen.

Writers and journalists were writing stories about them, many of them sensationalized trash, saying things like, "The steroids that he used previously made him test positive again," not knowing that Adderall is not a steroid. But people only read the headlines.

I went from being the golden boy to the poster child of doping in a matter of months. But two journalists really wanted to know the truth. These journalists were usually the skeptical ones who made it hard for athletes to get praise because they wanted to put the real truth out there. In the beginning, they were very skeptical of my court case, but as they dove into the story and read more about how everything transpired, they began to scratch their heads and realized that a lot of truths weren't being told.

But when they wrote their articles, they were pretty much silenced by their editors and the USADA and WADA. One journalist was actually transferred to a different location to silence her, and the other one was removed from the sports section. This played to the USADA and WADA's favor going into these court cases because there was nothing there for people to question. They were essentially only hearing one side.

My court proceedings would start with arbitration, held in Atlanta, Georgia. My agent, Renaldo Nehemiah, who had never been in this situation before, was helping along the way. I really thought that Renaldo was going to split. I was facing a lifetime ban, and why would he stay with someone who wasn't going to be able to make him money? But he did. He stayed, and he helped out through the whole process. And that's really when he became family to me.

The first lawyers that he brought to us were from a New York firm. Mind you, this was a very foreign situation to me. It felt like I was watching a movie of myself. As we spoke with the lawyers, I had the feeling that they weren't 100 percent on my side. I would explain what had happened, and they'd respond with a hollow nod or affirmation, like, "Yeah. Okay, great."

Before the arbitration began, my parents and I received a phone call from the New York firm. They said, "We got word from USADA that if you don't contest the science of your urine sample, they won't go for a lifetime ban. They'll reduce it to eight years."

Now, you need to realize that eight years out of the sport is like a lifetime ban. People's careers last for eight years. Being naive to the whole situation, we just felt like we were the good guys. We tried to cooperate as much as possible, even when it put our necks on the line, but we were disregarding common sense. We agreed not to contest the science, and they sent the word back that now I was facing eight years.

Then we got another phone call. The New York lawyer said, "Can you come to New York and meet us? We want to sit down with you and talk. We also have someone we want you to meet."

We went to their office in New York, and a tall, slender man walked in, Jeff Novitzky. Jeff was a straight shooter, a quiet guy, but he got to the point. He had discovered the BALCO scandal. He had been going through the trash outside of the BALCO company and found calendars, initials, and dates that didn't line up. When he started connecting the dots, he found out about this whole drug scandal that was happening.

Jeff had also seen that my coach was the one who had turned in a syringe with an undetectable designer drug in it. Now my coach considered himself a whistleblower. But the question always remained: where did you get it? And that question was never fully answered.

This prompted Jeff Novitzky to go down the rabbit hole and try to reverse engineer this drug scandal. I was the closest athlete to Trevor Graham and the most notable at that point in time since Marion Jones and Tim Montgomery had parted ways with him, so Jeff thought it would help his investigation to ask me questions and try to figure out exactly what my relationship with Trevor was.

After we had all been introduced, Jeff asked me, "Would you give Trevor a call? I have some questions written up that I want you to ask him, and I would like to hear how he responds."

My parents and I looked at each other. Then my parents said, "We need a moment to discuss this alone with our family." And we did. It only took us about five or six minutes, but we agreed. We didn't see any harm in doing that, especially if it was going to exonerate me. I didn't know anything, and I wasn't involved in anything, so we agreed and went forward.

Jeff was surprised by this. He said, "I've never had someone return that quickly and not be reluctant to do so."

"That's because I know I'm innocent," I replied. "I don't know anything, but I will help you as much as I can."

So, I called Trevor. Jeff had a series of questions lined up in front of me on paper that he wanted me to ask as he listened in on the conversation. It was an awkward conversation because I was asking Trevor questions about topics that he and I had never discussed before. "Do you know of a laboratory in Tampa? Do you know of this drug? Do you know of this time frame? Do you know these individuals?" I know the conversation sounded weird.

Trevor gave me nothing. You could almost feel him smirking a little bit on the phone. He just said, "I don't know what you're talking about, man." *This is not working*, I thought. *I'm not getting the information*. So, we ended the conversation.

Jeff scratched his head a little bit and said, "Are you willing to take a lie detector test?"

Once again, my parents and I looked at each other. But I agreed. "I have nothing to hide."

He pulled a polygraph device out of his bag, and it took him about 30 minutes to set up. Once again, I felt like I was in a movie or an episode of *Law & Order*. After I was strapped into this device, he asked me a series of questions. As I answered them, he would watch how the ink lines were jumping up and down on the paper. He finished the text and told me the results: I was telling the truth.

Now, I felt like I was on top of the world. I was innocent. I'd just proved that with this lie detector test. At that point, my case seemed like a slam dunk. "This kid knows nothing. He's a pawn. He's a victim."

But when you're dealing with the USADA and WADA, there are a lot of bylaws that say you are responsible for what goes into your body. That makes you the one who's ultimately responsible. I felt my situation was a little different. Their testing had determined that the drug had been delivered through a topical cream. It hadn't been injected or ingested. And the only time I'd ever had anything other than lotion put on my body was when Chris Webstein rubbed me down. That was how I was able to backtrack and figure out how I tested positive.

I laid out the scenario to my lawyers. When you get a massage, you lie on a table, usually face down. That's a part of the process. You don't know who is massaging you or what they are doing to your body. You're just lying there passively.

It made a lot of sense to me, but the lawyers didn't seem to believe me. And I feel like something was holding them back from really finding my freedom. And as we started getting closer to the arbitration, the lawyers started acting weird. One of them went on vacation and never came back. I felt like I was dead in the water. I didn't have a firm that was really working with me anymore.

But then Mr. Collins stepped in, the lawyer who helped me with my first case involving Adderall. He felt like he would be able to "fight the fight" for us, and he knew exactly what I was going through since he had helped with the first situation.

I was still facing eight years, but I felt like we had put together a strong case, strong enough to where athletes in a similar situation wouldn't be condemned. However, the arbitrator decided to split the baby. Instead of getting eight years, I was given four, which, again, was unheard of. No athlete in track and field had ever served a four-year ban. It was a long stretch of time, and I left feeling defeated. Even though I wasn't banned for life, which I was happy about, or even eight years, it still felt like a lifetime ban. Four years. I had a huge mountain in front of me to climb once again.

CHAPTER 12

# Purgatory: Part 3

As we tried to figure out how I could operate with this four-year ban, we received a letter in the mail. The WADA and IAAF immediately appealed the decision. They wanted eight years. They wanted to throw the book at me. I never felt more like a villain in my life than at that moment. No one wanted to see the writing on the wall. No one wanted to have the common sense to see that I had the pedigree. I'd been running and a champion since the moment I understood what running and racing were.

As we moved forward, I felt like Collins was starting to give me the same energy as the New York lawyers had, almost like he was thinking, *We can't defeat these monsters. We can't go toe to toe against USADA and WADA and win this case. It's impossible.* That was the vibe he was giving me.

So, we parted ways. Collins stepped back from being the head lawyer, and we were introduced to a California lawyer. This lawyer broke it down for us over the call, saying, "My group of smart lawyers and paralegals and I think that we can help you fight this case. I have no allegiance to the USADA or WADA. I'm working outside, operating as an individual." This impressed us, so we hired his firm.

We prepared ourselves for the CAS, or the Court of Arbitration for Sport, which was the next level. After you appeal, you go to the CAS, which is in New York City. I just remember being so depressed that I made myself sick. I literally caught the flu. I sat in that courtroom shivering and shaking because I was so sick and stressed out.

As the case proceeded, we discovered that we were no longer under New York City rules. The CAS was headquartered in Switzerland, and those were the rules we had to go by. I was told, "Consider yourself in Switzerland when we start this case."

The way that works is that three individuals sit at the front of the room. One individual is leaning towards my side of the story, one is leaning towards their side of the story, and then there's a neutral party who listens to both sides. They come together in the end to make a decision that they feel is fair.

We sat there for the next couple of days, listening to the CAS and pleading our case. It was so long and drawn out to the point where one of the three individuals sitting up front was falling asleep while trying to listen to my story, a story that was going to save my life. I felt disrespected. I felt like no one was taking me seriously, and no one wanted to know exactly what really happened to me.

Then a gentleman walked in, and his name was Joe Zarzaur. Joe is from Pensacola, my hometown, and he came highly recommended by a family friend. He is a bulldog lawyer who thinks outside the box. Once he has a scent, he won't stop tracking until he finds what he's looking for.

As the proceedings continued, we entered the discovery phase. In discovery, you find out what information your opponent has, and you share your information. That is when we found out why they didn't want us to contest the science of the urine sample. According to protocol within their rules and guidelines, if you're taking a urine sample from an athlete or a group of athletes, you seal it up and put it in a travel bag, and it's not to be opened until it gets to the laboratory. A courier travels with this bag, and they have to document if anything happens along the way. They had evidence that this courier reported that the bag was opened and tampered with during transportation to the laboratory. Their rules state if anything happens to this bag, all samples must be thrown out. Right there in black and white. The case should have ended right there, but it didn't. They broke their own rules.

We also found out through the CAS that other individuals were testing positive for other medications and drugs that were illegal in every state, like cocaine, and they were getting warnings. This made me wonder if they were targeting me. Did racism have something to do with it? The thought made me even more depressed.

When I left that courtroom, the result was the same: four years, nothing more and nothing less. Nothing changed. I felt like I was in purgatory. I felt like I was isolated. I felt defeated, but Joe had something up his sleeve.

I went back to Pensacola and didn't do much with my life. I was partying hard every night and drinking with friends. Sometimes, I'd drink around ten Jägerbombs in a row. I was doing all the wrong things, things that were definitely not me, even driving drunk. I just had so much disregard for everything. I had so much pain in my heart. I didn't feel like I wanted to end my life, but I didn't feel like my life meant anything anymore. So, I put myself in dangerous situations and didn't really care. One time, I said, "If I wrapped my car around this telephone pole right now, no one would miss me." I cried myself to sleep every night.

But I did feel safe in Pensacola. I felt safe because these were the people who cheered me on and clapped for me when I won the gold medal. If I couldn't be safe there, I couldn't be safe anywhere.

I had a big customized truck, a Cadillac Escalade, and I parked it outside of my house. One morning, around eight o'clock, our doorbell rang. My mom was already up, getting ready to go out and run errands in town. She answered the door, and our neighbor to the left of us was standing there, holding his son in his arms, and he said, "I think someone messed with your truck. I think you should come check it out. It's on the side of your truck." Now, the side of the truck he was talking about faced his house. My mom became frantic and told me, "Go see what he's talking about, Justin."

I went outside and saw that someone had written something on my truck with a marker like the ones kids use for homecoming. It just said "steroids." I instantly became embarrassed, and to this day, I remember the look on that neighbor's face, a mix of worry, embarrassment, and anxiousness. You could tell that he didn't want to deliver this news. It hurt him.

I just removed my shirt and used it to wipe off the "steroids" written on the side of my truck as much as I could. Then I went back into the house. My mom asked me, "What was he talking about?"

"Nothing, Mom," I told her. "Just don't worry about it."

I went into my room and cried into a pillow. I didn't feel safe anymore anywhere. It was a tough situation to be in. The only way I was able to escape it was to keep drinking, so I partied harder.

Then we got a call from Joe Zarzaur. He said, "I was looking into your case, and I was thinking about how you've been treated, about your whole career. After doing some research, it's my opinion that you should never have served time for your offense. You have ADD, a disability that you've taken medication for since you were a child. I think that I can help you win this case by thinking outside of the box." Then he added, "And I don't work for the pooling system created by the USADA."

"What do you mean?" I asked. He explained that when you tested positive, and you'd see it in the emails and letters they sent you, the organizations referred you to a pool of lawyers who could help you because they were well-versed in these cases, which you would feel was very obliging, as you didn't have to go out there and find lawyers who had to read up and study the bylaws. But these lawyers were in bed with the USADA. At the end of the year, the USADA would take them on retreats. The same lawyers fighting for athletes' lives and sitting with us in the courtroom were being wined and dined by the organizations they were competing against in court. They were in bed with each other.

When I heard that, I felt that the energy I had sensed from the New York lawyers and from Collins after a while was because they were limited.

They could not win. They weren't trying to win. All they were trying to do was make sure that they got their money and were able to be as successful as possible while the athletes they represented served their time.

I'd spent over half a million dollars in court proceedings. My life felt like it had gone down the drain. But then Joe came back into the picture. He said, "I'm going to think outside the box, and I'm going to do something that is definitely going to shake up the world."

He brought a case against the USADA using the Americans with Disabilities Act. He wanted to take it, in his words, "out of this kangaroo court system," so we had the case in Pensacola, which was his home turf. The Americans with Disabilities Act protects all Americans with disabilities, both physical and mental, including those with ADD and ADHD. Given that I was clinically diagnosed with ADD at an early age, I should have been protected from this type of ban and scrutiny.

Once again, the USADA came into the courtroom on the first day with around ten lawyers. And they had all of these heavy boxes filled with papers and filings. The judge said to them, "This is what you guys are doing? You're bringing ten lawyers in here with all of these boxes just for this one guy? You should be ashamed of yourself."

Joe put on a great show and made very valid points. He continued to push the disability act so that we could sue USADA for this entire situation and receive financial compensation. We won! In the history of court proceedings with USADA, no one has ever won in this way. We won, and my family and I received financial compensation for damages. It was my first real victory in a while, and I needed that.

There was one condition: I was not legally allowed to discuss the details of the case until the day I retired from the sport. They feared that if the public knew about this, others who had experienced a similar ban might try the same strategy of suing. For the rest of my career, one thought always sat in the back of my head: *The people who write these terrible stories and lies about me don't know what the truth is. And I can't speak about it until I retire.*

Joe also hoped that from this, we would be able to reduce the length of the ban and get me back on the track. However, our request was denied, so I had to sit out the rest of my time and not compete.

I lost sponsorships. I lost everything. Imagine not being able to earn a living for two years, five years, and possibly more. I didn't make a living for over half a decade. I was so depressed, but I still had to keep a smile on my face. I still had to stay strong for my parents because they felt the same way: depressed. My dad talked less. My mom started stressing out and losing hair. It was a hard situation. And me living at home wasn't helping. I told my parents, "I need to get up and move. I need to do something. I need to be ready when I get out from under this suspension."

CHAPTER 13

# Purgatory: Part 4

S tarting a football career became a possibility. There were some trainers in Atlanta, Georgia, who wanted me, so I moved there. I stayed with my aunt and uncle for a couple of months as I trained. I drove almost an hour to practice each day. It was a different feeling. Atlanta was a different feeling, too. It felt more dangerous. I needed to stay on my toes.

Around that time, I was sitting in a bar with a friend, watching the 2008 Olympics, the 100-meter finals. Usain Bolt won the race in grand fashion, bigger and better than anybody I'd ever seen before, beating his chest 20 meters out before he crossed the finish line and smashing the world record.

For most people, this would have been intimidating, or they might have thought, *I can't go back now. I can't compete against him.* But I just remember sitting on that bar stool, looking up at that TV, and saying, "I want to race that guy one day. And I want to do it when he's at his best." I stuck that in the back of my mind as I trained for football.

I got invited to a couple of practices. I went to visit the New Orleans Saints at their facility, where I was introduced to Sean Payton. He said, "I'm going to train you today," and we went through different routes, cuts, and steps. We were the only ones on the field—me and him. Then he looked at me and said, "Now we're going to make sure that you can catch. We're going to get somebody to throw some balls at you."

Out of the facility walked Drew Brees. I was just beside myself. I couldn't believe that I was running routes with the Saints and catching passes from Drew Brees.

After practice, I went back to the locker, and as I was taking my equipment off, I noticed a guy standing nearby. I looked over at him, and it was Reggie Bush. I thought, *Man, this is a dream come true.*

From that point on, I was on a football cycle. I did private practices for the Titans. I did private practices for the Arizona Cardinals. And then I got a call from a football agent, who said, "You got invited to the Bucs minicamp."

I went down to Tampa and stayed there for about a week and a half at their minicamp. It was so different. It was a gauntlet. We had two-a-day practices in almost 90-degree weather. We had to run routes spontaneously, and plays were thrown at us from all different angles. We got a playbook on the first day, and it had ten plays in it.

Now, I looked like a football player. I moved like a football player. I could catch the ball like a football player, and I could run routes like a football player. But as I sat there in my bed until one o'clock in the morning, studying the ten plays they'd given us, I could only memorize about five of them. I told myself, "I'm not going to remember all of them, but I'm going to remember five for sure, and it's going to be a 50-50 shot." And that's exactly how the practice unfolded. On some plays, I did really well, and on others, it was like, "What are you doing out there, Justin?"

We gathered to watch the highlight films, and Jon Gruden, who was the head coach for the Bucs at the time, said, "Gold medal"—he called me "Gold Medal"—"what are you doing out there, man? You need to get better."

So, I told myself, *I'm going to get better. I'm going to go back to the room tonight, I'm going to read the other five plays, I'm going to memorize them, and I'm going to be perfect. I'm going to be ready.* But before we left that meeting, they gave us another notebook with ten more plays in it. I felt like I was overwhelmed. I was up until five o'clock in the morning trying to memorize plays, only to get up at seven o'clock in the morning to get ready for practice. The whole time, my roommate slept like a baby.

Sitting there one night with the lamp on, I looked up at the ceiling and said, "Why am I trying so hard to be a normal athlete in a world where they don't believe in track and field athletes? I need to go back to the sport where I once was a king. At least I know how to rule there."

That night, I decided to go back into track and field. It was a brave decision because people who try to make a comeback in track and field often find it a lonely road, especially when drugs are involved. But I planned to go back and be as brave as possible.

I trained with a coach named Eric Campbell. Coach Campbell was in Atlanta, and he was the only one I knew who would train me at that time. No one else wanted to touch me with a ten-foot pole, but he trained me hard. I worked with people who had regular jobs. They would come after work to train. I found that very admirable. Coach Campbell trained me for a couple of months, and I worked really hard. We trained in very rugged terrain, in places like city parks and broken-down railroad tracks. We trained wherever we could.

Then my agent reached out to me and said, "Would you consider working with Lawrence Seagraves and Raina Ryder over in Marietta, Georgia?" At the time, I was in Duluth, an hour away.

I told my agent, "I'll drive to the moon and back. I'll sacrifice everything to get back on that track and get with a good system." And that's what I did. It was an hour's drive to and from practice, but as I started to train, I was amongst some of the greats of track and field, and they embraced me: Angelo Taylor, Dwight Phillips, Daniel Carruthers, Perdita Felicien, Walter Davis, Travis Padgett, and George Kitchens. All of these people had made names for themselves. This was probably one of the best training groups I've ever been in with respect to talent. As I trained, I remembered that it was about sacrifice, about taking the time to be the best athlete I could be. No one was on that bull with me.

I was overweight: 210 pounds, when I should have been around 180. The guys gave me a nickname. I went from being Justin Gatlin to Justin "Fatlin." I knew it was a little bit endearing, but it was also a wake-up call. If I wanted to achieve my goals, I had to get right. I couldn't be heavy. So, I started to change that narrative.

One day, I came to practice a little earlier than usual, and one of my teammates was already there in the parking lot. He didn't see me, but I was surprised that he was already there. He got out of his car, went to his trunk, and opened it, and I saw that he had everything in it, like his whole house was in his trunk. This guy was living out of his car. I hadn't realized the sacrifice he was making for this dream to happen. It showed me how precious it was for everybody in this situation. Everyone was struggling in some way, shape, or form. This kid ended up going from having nothing to qualifying for the Olympic team. It was a beautiful moment, one that taught me that if you just give all you have in this moment, the moment can be yours.

I felt that same energy coming from Coach Loren Seagrave, like he was shoulder to shoulder with me, trying to conquer the world. He was a little standoffish, though, and that was not what I needed. I was used to having a coach who was there and present with me.

As we went forward, I had a couple of meets lined up around the world. The first was in Finland, and my mom wanted to go with me. "Mom," I said, "what do you mean? The only times you ever went to a meet was at the World Championships or the Olympics."

She said, "I know, but I'm worried about you."

So, we went to the meet together, me, Coach Loren, and my mom. It was my first 100-meter race after being gone from the scene, but it wasn't paying much, barely enough for my plane ticket to get over there. I was making less than peanuts.

Before the race, I thought, *Just compete. Just compete.* But when the gun went off, I felt like I was home again. I was racing again. I came across the line victorious. I had won my first race back. My time was 10.24 seconds, which was a lot slower than my previous 9.7s, 9.8s, and 9.9s, but it was a starting point.

I finished that season racing at all of these hole-in-the-wall meets around the world, not really making any money. It was kind of like practice to get back to where I needed to be. I knew that I needed a different type of training, so my agent reached out to other coaches. This began my return to track and field.

We will all face setbacks in our lives. This will happen on your mission to success. Some setbacks will be more difficult or devastating than others. As you can see, I have had my fair share. But I refuse to let that define me, and so should you. You can be *down,* but always practice never being *out.* The lowest point in my life transformed me into the toughest person in my life. If you can overcome the toughest moments of your life, how you mold your life afterward will become easier.

This is the time to have a talk with yourself. Follow my **Three Best Practices** below:

- Make a list of your worst-case scenarios that could happen to you in your life.
- Make a list of plans to prepare and go through those steps in your mind.
- With growing success also comes increased challenges.
  - Remember: "When we pray for rain, sometimes we have to deal with the mud too."
  - It will not be as easy as you think.
  - With the right mental preparation, you can strategically overcome any given situation.

CHAPTER 14

# Feather of a Phoenix: Part 1

I packed my bags and spikes for the move from Atlanta to Kissimmee, Florida. Kissimmee would be a whole different environment. Before leaving Atlanta, I was given an unexpected gift: the birth of my son, Jace Alexander Gatlin. His arrival meant the world to me, bringing joy back into my life and filling the hole in my heart. He gave me drive and passion, and this fueled me even more to find a better coach, a better scenario, a better training group so I could provide for Jace and he wouldn't have to want for anything in this world. I also wanted to make him proud to carry the Gatlin name. Moving was a tough decision for me, though, as it meant I would be leaving him in Atlanta. It hurt me for many years to have to deal with that.

In Kissimmee, I was being coached by Coach Brooks Johnson. Coach Johnson was legendary. He'd coached many Olympians, all the way back to the 50s and 60s, and was part of a coaching legacy that had transformed what American track and field looked like. He was no-nonsense, telling it like it is, but his straightforwardness was funny to me even when he was being serious. He would always call you by your last name until he respected you enough to call you by your first name.

I was with a group of athletes who were on the rise and making names for themselves: David Oliver, Novlene Mills, Joel Brown, and Dwight Thomas, to name a few. Everyone was excited about racing and competing around the world, but I soon realized I wasn't getting as many races as they were. Even though I did the time and faced the punishment, I was still being blackballed by the system. A lot of promoters and elites did not want to invite me. Once again, I was stuck. I was training more than I was competing, and this climb out of darkness was a tough situation for me.

I was able to qualify for the 2011 Daegu World Championships in Korea. I hit a qualifying mark and then made it to nationals. Nationals was going to be where I broke out. Coach Brooks and I discussed how we were going to operate and move. We diligently worked on my starts and running for months. When I finally got to that starting line and then made my way from prelims to semis to finals, I remembered his instruction.

We got into our set positions, and the gun went off. I took off running, and in the last meter, I started to celebrate. I roared and threw my hands out. I couldn't believe I was winning this race. It was an amazing feeling. And I did it from lane two. But Walter Dix, who was in lane six, was leaning and dove for the line. He beat me by a shoulder. I was shocked because this was usually the move that I did. I'd sneak past people at the finish line and win.

I went back to the warm-up area, and the first thing Coach Brooks said to me was, "A meter. You ran 99 meters. You still owe me a meter." He said it with a serious expression, but then he gave me a little smirk. "Don't you ever do that again. We come to win."

As we went forward, everything started to unfold. I was in a championship mentality now. No one could deny my greatness. No one could say, "You can't come to this meet," or "You can't run in this lane." I earned that spot. I had earned my place on that team.

But as we trained that next month, getting ready for the World Championships, I quickly realized that I'd forgotten how hot Florida was. We were training in 90-degree weather. That was when I was introduced to the cryotherapy chamber. A replacement for ice baths, it uses dry ice and different forms of chemicals, so it's not as messy. The first time I used it, I stepped into the chamber right after practice, still wearing my sweat-soaked socks and tights. Mind you, you were supposed to take off as much clothing as possible before entering the chamber. And you were only supposed to stay in it for two minutes, which should tell you how strong this thing is.

But I couldn't even finish those two minutes. After being in there for only a minute, my skin started to burn, especially on my legs and ankles. I ran out of the chamber and raced around the therapy room because my whole body felt like it was on fire. I soon found out that you can't wear damp clothes in the chamber because they will freeze, causing instant frostbite.

As I bent over to take off my socks, I noticed icicles on my tights. I knew that was a bad sign. Then, when I peeled my socks off, a layer of skin came off with them. I had suffered frostbite in the summertime in Florida. This derailed my training. I had bruises and blisters, and my ankles and Achilles tendons were in constant pain. I couldn't train at the high level that I needed to.

Nevertheless, I am a determined individual. I wrapped my blisters and bruises up with athletic tape, not caring that I had to rip this tape off later. It was all about the training. So, as I got ready for the World Championships, I was in the medical room in Daegu, Korea, every day. Team USA was there in the morning, and those doctors and trainers were popping the blisters on my feet and Achilles tendons and then putting on baby powder and gauze to try to dry out the burns. I would wrap my feet and ankles with athletic tape and then go out and compete.

I made it through the prelims, but I was in agony the whole time. In the village, I walked around with flip-flops on, almost barefoot, because I couldn't put any pressure on my blisters and burns. But I knew that if I wanted to make it to the next round, I had to prepare myself for the pain. In the semis, I faltered. The pain was just too much, and I didn't make it to the finals. This was the first championship where I didn't make it to the finals, let alone make it onto the podium. I had to sit in pain and just watch the finals.

CHAPTER 15

# Feather of a Phoenix: Part 2

As I healed myself and prepared for the next season, I realized that something was missing: I didn't have adequate training partners. In other words, I didn't have a sprinter to spar with, to sharpen myself with, something I was used to having throughout college and my professional career. I was training amongst 400-meter runners and hurdlers. It was a very difficult time because I didn't know where my potential was. I didn't know if I was in good shape or not because I was training by myself the whole time.

I told my agent that I needed a change, so we started to look for training partners. Unfortunately, I was still toxic. No one wanted to touch me with a ten-foot pole. And with Coach Brooks being who he was, a taskmaster, a lot of athletes didn't want to deal with him, either. I was stuck in a situation where I was training with athletes who were not on my level of talent, and it just wasn't working out, so I had to have a conversation with Coach Brooks. When I went to his house to tell him how I felt, I was almost shaking. I was so nervous. I sat in his office and, while looking down at the hat I was balling up in my hands, said, "I think that we're going to have to part ways because we can't find anybody that I can train with who will give me the competition that I need."

"Justin," he said, "you came into this group, and before you were even making any money at all, you paid me. You still don't have a contract, but you found a way to pay me in full. I respect you. I respect the athlete you are, and most importantly, I respect the son you are to your parents." After giving me his blessing, he pointed me in the direction of Dennis Mitchell, who was literally just across town in Clermont, Florida.

I did some research on Dennis, and my agent started corresponding with him. One night, we connected, and he looked me in my eyes and said, "I have a stable, but I don't have that horse that I'm looking for."

I took a sip of my beer and replied, "I'm a horse, and I don't have a stable."

At that moment, we both thought, *This is going to work out perfectly.*

I paid the bill, we shook hands, and he told me, "I'll see you at practice tomorrow."

I was so excited. I packed my bags, drove across town, got to practice early, did the whole interview, and met my teammates. I was ready to train. I was ready to compete. The first thing we worked on was my start. He said, "You're in a different era now. This is not the era where you can run people down like you used to. You've got to have a start. These athletes out here not only run 9.7s, but they're running 9.5s and 9.6s. This is something that you've never experienced before, and neither have I. But I know that if we get into the party, we can cut the rug."

The way to get into the party was by becoming the best starter in the world. Mind you, I'd never been a great starter. I was an average starter, but I had a high top speed. What really helped me was the fact that Dennis was a technique master. We would have regular practice for about an hour and a half, and then he would stay another hour with me after practice and work on my start. As we worked on it, he would say, "Nope, try it again. Nope, try it again."

Then I had a great idea. I asked him, "Why don't we try out our start in real competition? Maybe I should run indoors."

"I don't believe in indoors," he said, "but if you're going to run indoors and we're going to make this team, we're going to go out there, and we're going to win, and we're going to get the gold medal.

"All right, Coach," I said. "You're speaking my language."

As we prepared for the 2012 Indoor World Championships in Istanbul, we got a lot of looks. People stared at me like I was a ghost. They couldn't believe I was back on the scene. A lot of people hated the fact that I was competing again. But I was victorious once again. I came across the finish line first, beating some of the best starters in the world in the process.

I'd finally gotten another world title under my belt after a long time away from the sport. I felt like I had arrived. In 2012, almost nine years later, I won with the same time that I had in the 2003 World Championships: 6.45 seconds.

CHAPTER 16

# Feather of a Phoenix: Part 3

This is the point where you say hello to the bad guy.

I say that because the media had a field day with me. Usually, when an athlete tests positive, they become a shell of the person they are. The proof is in the pudding. If they were really using drugs and stopped using them, they're not out there competing at a high level anymore. But I was doing the opposite. I was still running and competing at a high level. I was proving myself.

But they were still running these sensational stories: "If you pump someone full of drugs, they'll be in their system for years," "Justin Gatlin is a lab rat." "Justin Gatlin is a two-time doper." "Justin Gatlin is all of these negative things." Never once did they mention my prior successes, like that I was an Olympic gold medalist. My title became "two-time doper" in almost every article I read. It turned me off to the point of not wanting to read articles anymore, especially about myself, even if they were good.

We worked so hard to get a sponsorship, but no one was stepping up to the plate—not Nike, not Adidas, nobody. I was still toxic. So, my agent thought outside the box. He started looking for sponsors overseas, and one rang a bell: Xtep. Xtep was a company in China worth ten million dollars. Models and movie stars promoted them, but I was the first real athlete who had ever thought of signing with them.

We took a trip to China, and as I sat in the office of Mr. Ding, president and CEO of Xtep, I said, "I promise you, sir, I'm going to bring an Olympic medal to you. I'm going to change the narrative of what the company represents." He was very happy, and he actually gave me more creative control over what the uniforms would look like. I stood out in front of everybody. I was the only athlete signed to Xtep. I loved it. I felt like an individual again, and I felt like I finally had a team behind me again.

In 2012, I was ready for the Olympic trials. I was hungry. Once again, I had a uniform, I had a team, and I had a company behind me, but Xtep didn't make spikes. They only made shoes for marathon runners, so we had to make some. They ended up giving me "Franken-spikes," where the upper parts of the shoes were grafted onto spike plates. Unfortunately, they used low-quality materials, so whenever I sweat, the logo would come off. I was constantly patching them up, but I did it with pride because I knew nobody else wanted me out there. They did, and I was going to represent them when I stepped out onto the track. So, in my spike bag, I carried my spike key, some extra spikes, my track cleats, and a large stock of superglue to make sure that my logo stayed on and my spike plates didn't separate from the uppers—basically so that my shoes didn't explode at top speed.

During the Olympic trials, I was being interviewed, and the reporter kept asking me a whole bunch of negative questions. I replied, "At this point, do the math, I'm needed. There's not an American athlete who's able to battle against Usain Bolt, Yohan Blake, and the Jamaican athletes taking over the sprint game right now. So, consider me Batman." The reporters all got quiet because they understood exactly where I was coming from.

The difference between Dennis Mitchell and Loren Seagrave is the fact that Dennis instilled fire in you. He wanted to go to war with you. The morning of the trials, we marched down into the lobby, got on the bus, went to the track, and walked together as I warmed up. He would constantly whisper to me, "We're going out there to handle business. This is war. These guys don't have anything on you. You are the man. You're going to step up to this plate, and you're going to handle business. So, let's do this." Then we parted ways, and I went into the call room to get ready for the 100-meter race. But I remembered those words. I remembered who I was. I won. I was back on top, the most dominant sprinter in America once again.

But to backtrack for a minute, before I got into the finals, my spikes were not up to par. So, we came up with the idea of having a carve-out in our contract where I could use Nike spikes instead of Xtep spikes. Xtep was okay with it because they didn't officially have spikes, and Nike was all for it as well. They even paid me for that carve-out. Nike didn't want to see Justin Gatlin win the Olympic 100-meter trials without a swoosh on him. It messed with their ego, so they paid me well for nine seconds of wearing their shoes.

But that was off the table going into the Olympics. I was back in the Xtep spikes. During the 2012 Olympics in London, I had to sit in the tent in between rounds and superglue my Xtep "Franken-spikes" together. My coach would say, "Your spikes are going to explode halfway through this race." Then he'd chuckle and shake his head.

The finals turned out to be one of the most epic races in track and field history. Halfway through the race, I was actually winning. I was in front of Usain Bolt, the guy I had watched from a bar in 2008 win the Olympics, and I thought the moment had arrived where I would be able to say, "I beat this guy." I gave it my all, but when the dust settled, he had won the race with a time of 9.6 seconds. Yohan Blake came in second with a 9.7, and I finished third with a 9.7 as well. There I was, back on the Olympic podium. It wasn't the finish I'd wanted, but it was a great starting point for my return to the track.

As they called my name and put the bronze medal around my neck, the crowd cheered and celebrated. I received so much love, and I was back. I was the man again. I was in the best shape of my life.

CHAPTER 17

# Feather of a Phoenix: Part 4

After the Olympics, I had a few more races in Europe. I knew that I could run much faster than I was, and I was ready to do so. But then, on an early morning flight, I ate a sandwich, and everything changed. I got food poisoning, the worst I'd ever had in my life. This brought back that fear I'd always had of being stuck in Europe, where I couldn't communicate properly. But now I had succumbed to this food poisoning and was stuck in my room for at least a day and a half, throwing up, unable to hold anything down.

The trainer who was with me didn't know what to do at all. She just kept bringing food to the room. I would drift in and out of sleep, and when I woke up, there would be a large pizza, a bag of McDonald's, or a basket of fruit waiting for me. She brought me anything and everything, almost as if she were praying to me like a deity.

Eventually, they saw that I was really sick. I was wearing two pairs of pants, two pairs of tube socks, three shirts, a hoodie, and a skully (knit cap), with every blanket and sheet in the room on top of me, but I still was shivering. I also had a bad fever. When they took me to the hospital, I couldn't even walk. They had to roll me through the doors in a wheelchair. They took me down a long hallway that ended with huge metal doors. The doors opened to reveal an operating room, and I thought, *Oh, my God. They're about to operate on me.* Thankfully, that didn't end up happening.

The doctors diagnosed me with food poisoning, gave me some medication, and sent me on my way. Over time, I got better, but that episode ended my 2012 season because I lost a lot of strength and speed. I just had to get ready for the 2013 season.

I was a different person in 2013, more confident and happy. However, I was still blackballed from a lot of Diamond League meets, and the Diamond League put on most of the high-profile meets around the world.

The meet in Rome, Italy, was my first time going up against Usain Bolt in a one-off race. Now, mind you, I'd watched him and studied him since 2012, how he ran and competed. Only one person had ever beaten him: his teammate and training partner Yohan Blake. I studied Yohan's style and technique, and I was in awe of the fact that though he was only five foot ten, shorter than me, he was able to beat someone who was six foot five. He created power in a different way and was working on his step-down techniques.

I tried to emulate that in my 2013 race in Rome. The gun went off, and I ran shoulder to shoulder with Usain. Now, Usain's style was to take off at 45 to 50 meters and decimate the field. But as he started to take off and leave everyone in the dust, I stayed right next to him, stride for stride, all the way to the finish line. I dove for that finish line and beat him.

When we came across that line, the whole stadium was in disbelief, but they still cheered. It was crazy. I looked at Usain as he looked up at the scoreboard and realized that he'd lost. All he did was shrug as if to say, "Oh, well. I guess it just wasn't my day."

Afterward, at the press conference, I was so happy. I was asked really good questions, really positive questions. When it was over, I was walking out, and Usain Bolt and his agent were in front of me, close enough for me to hear their conversation. Usain leaned over to his agent and said, "That was so embarrassing. That's never happening again." I never raced Usain Bolt in a one-off race anywhere in the world ever again. The only time I would meet him would be in the finals of championship races. I think he realized that the more he raced me, the more I was able to use that to beat him, something that neither he nor his coach wanted.

The next time I raced Usain was at the World Championships in Moscow, Russia. Usain lit that race up. In front of the world, he put on a great show. A thunderstorm swept through right before the finals. The wind was blowing so hard that the tents seemed about to pull up their stakes and blow away. Lightning lit up the sky, and rain poured down. We were the last event, so the officials were literally packing up their bags as Usain and I went into the call room to get ready to run. We were like two gladiators battling in the elements. In the end, he won that race, but it was okay because I knew exactly what I needed to work on to get better.

The next year was an off year, meaning no Olympics and no World Championships. It just was time to compete in races around the world, have a good time, and make some money. These races could be dogfights, though. I went into 2014 with so much confidence that I was undefeated for the whole season. I did not lose one race in either the 100 or the 200, and I won the Diamond League Trophy, my second.

Keep in mind the Diamond League had blackballed me. I couldn't run in most of the races, but I still won back-to-back trophies. My coach and I said, "If you're going to blackball at the end of the season, we're going to frontload the beginning of the season." That's exactly what we did, and I won all the races at the beginning of the season, at least three or four in a row. This put me so far ahead of everyone else that no one could catch me. For someone to surpass me, they would have had to win every other race in the season.

I started winning more races and receiving more bonuses, and I became so successful that my Xtep couldn't keep up with my contract. Now I had a tough decision to make: should I stay with a company that might terminate me because my price point was becoming too high, or should I walk away from them and start a new chapter with someone else?

Around this time, Dennis Mitchell became a Nike coach, which was very exciting for him because he had worked really hard for that as well. And since I now had a Nike coach, Nike decided to play hardball knowing that my contract was up with Xtep. They put a number on the table, but I knew I was worth significantly more. They said "If you want Dennis to be your coach, you have to take this number. Otherwise, you walk away from both."

They left me with no choice. I had to take the offer. I just made sure that whenever I ran, I competed to the best of my abilities.

The path to success is never a straight line. With all my achievements, obstacles were still thrown in my path. I learned you cannot have one without the other, so I prepared for sunny days *and* rainy days. With this preparation, I was ready to conquer the world. While focusing on your mission, be vigilant and aware of your surroundings. This is critical for your success and consistency. Celebrating is for the ones who are finished. If you are not finished, stay focused and hungry. It is OK to acknowledge your progress and small victories. It is great to win small battles, but you are here to *win the war*. At times, I would look back at my small victories and break down the process of how I obtained them. Every moment is a checkpoint in your mission. Become obsessed with the details and see the moments.

---

Here are six powerful reminders to carry with you every day:

- Be aware of the environment you are operating in.
- Assess and understand the situation around you and learn to thrive in the chaos.
- Remind yourself why you are pursuing your goals.
- Analyze your wins and losses.
- Always keep your eye on the end game.
- Never stop checking in with yourself.

CHAPTER 18

# Body Over Mind: Part 1

After finishing the 2014 season undefeated, I had a different mentality going into 2015. I wanted to do more. I wanted to beat the Jamaicans. I wanted to get to the level they were at. I wanted to dominate again. I wanted to bring championships and glory back to Team USA.

As I started my season, I focused on everything that had been limiting me: the way I trained, the way I lifted in the gym, the way I pulled sleds, the way I recovered, my mindset, everything. Instead of treating training as just something I clocked in and clocked out of every day, I made it my lifestyle. I ate differently. I became more regimented. Whether I was pulling a sled with 45 pounds on it or benching a certain weight, I pushed myself to go beyond that limit. I forged my body into a weapon, into a machine, to be unbeatable. At times, I would work out with the team and then circle back around and go work out for another hour in the gym. I wanted to be undefeated again, and everything was working as planned.

My first race of the season was in Doha, Qatar. It was on my son's birthday, May 11. As I got in the blocks, I whispered to myself the time I wanted to run: "9.7 seconds, 9.7 seconds, 9.7 seconds." When the gun fired, I took off like a rocket and left everyone in my wake. As I came across the finish line, I looked up and saw *"9.73 seconds,"* one of the fastest times in human history. I was so excited that I jumped into the stands. I couldn't have been happier.

The win was a great start to my 2015 campaign. I put everyone on notice in track and field, especially male sprinters: "I'm here, and I'm going to be a problem to deal with this season." As the season went on, Usain had a whole different vibe. He was having probably one of the worst seasons of his career, whereas I was having one of the best seasons of my life.

I was running 9.7s like they were going out of style. I ran five 9.7s in that season, which was unheard of. No athlete had ever done that before. I found my rhythm, and I was able to align it with my hunger. It was harder for me to run slow than it was for me to run fast.

I felt like a superhero, and I became somewhat of a nightmare. My reputation preceded me. When I showed up at a meet, everyone looked at me as if they were seeing a ghost. I would hear people whisper things like, "Well, I guess I'm getting second today." They saw how unbeatable I had become. I wasn't going to let anything get in my way.

Because I had been so successful the last couple of years and had won the Diamond League Trophy in 2014, I got a bye for the 100 meters in the World Championships, which meant I didn't have to run to qualify. I was already on the team. That gave me the space to go out there and run the 200 meters at Nationals.

In 2014, my undefeated season, I had only run the 200 meters once (in Monaco) against a star-studded lineup. But it didn't mean anything to me more than it made me some money and drew an audience. For a long time, Dennis didn't want me to run 200s. He felt like I was becoming an older athlete and just needed to focus on the 100. Although I trained for the 200, I only raced it that one time.

In Monaco, Dennis walked me through the strategy of how to win the race from lane seven, and it worked. I won. But it was the ugliest race I've ever won. I bounced down the track from left to right like the ball in a pinball machine. Somehow, though, I ran the fastest time I'd ever run for the 200. I hadn't done that in the 200 since college, and my PR at that time was 19.86. In Monaco, my time was 19.68. I knew I had arrived and that I had done something very special. I was shocked, my coach was shocked, and the world was shocked as well.

I talked Dennis into letting me run the 200 in 2015, and he reluctantly agreed. He saw how it could work out. As I prepared for Nationals, I also prepared to run faster than I ever had in the 200. A bonus was that understanding the rhythm of the 200 helped me become a better 100-meter runner as well. At Nationals, I made it through the prelims and semis and into the finals.

I had a teammate, Isaiah Young, who trained with me. He'd told me straight up before the season started, "I'm going to do whatever you do. So, however hard you work, however much weight you squat, I'm right there next to you." I appreciated that because I'd always felt like a lone wolf. Now I had someone who understood how hard I was working.

Through those rounds for the 200, Isaiah and I laughed and had a great time. In the prelims, I asked him, "Are you going to run 19 seconds?"

He laughed and said, "We'll see what happens." Then he went out there and ran 19 seconds in the semis. He was on fire. I was very proud of him. But I knew I had a trick up my sleeve because I had the superior power at that point in time.

When the finals came around, I let it all hang out. I came around that turn in the lead. And in the straightaway, I kept pulling away, inching away from the competitors further and further. I crossed the finish line in 19.57 seconds, a time that hadn't been seen by an American athlete in a while. Isaiah finished under 20 seconds, too. I was very happy and excited, and I knew I was in the best shape of my life. Everyone was impressed with my 200-meter time, and I couldn't wait for them to see my next 100-meter time.

CHAPTER 19

# Body Over Mind: Part 2

The only thing left in sight was the 2015 World Championships in Beijing, China. As I prepared, I felt unstoppable, and a lot of the fans felt the same way. It was surreal, people coming over to me in the warm-up area and whispering, "Please, win this world championship. You can beat Bolt." I mean, everybody, from Team USA to runners from developing countries, wanted to see a different champion. No one wanted to speak out about it, but everybody wanted to tell me that I could be the one to dethrone him. It was an eerie feeling, being the favorite. I hadn't felt that for years. But this was what I'd been wanting. This was what I'd been praying for. This was what I'd been training for, to be number one. Now I wanted to go out there and seal the deal.

I got through my first round in the 100 meters easily. I ran with minimal effort and was able to clock a sub-10. But the semis were different. I felt like I could go out there and run my PR. Next to me was Mike Rogers, a younger athlete who ran for Team USA. We'd been on teams together for years. I understood that everyone was out there pushing to be the best and wanting to be the best and beat the best. As we raced, he competed like he was running the finals. He wanted to win that heat, but I wouldn't let him. We came across the line, and I'd run a 9.77. I felt like I'd used a little too much energy, but it was okay. I still felt amazing.

In Usain's semi, as he got off the blocks, he stumbled forward, and the crowd gasped because now he would probably finish in third place. Two young athletes who were on fire that season, Trayvon Bromell and Andre De Grasse, were in front of him. They were running stride for stride with each other, trying to put the big giant away. But Usain regained his composure, and with that long stride, he ran these young guys down to come across the finish line first. I thought, *Okay, he's ready to go*. He had a couple of falters but still came across the line in 9.8 seconds.

I knew that this was my moment. I felt strong. My inner circle was there, my coach and my training partners, and they were rooting for me. As we walked into the stadium for the final race of the 100 meters, the atmosphere was electric. I was ready. I settled in the blocks and raised my hips to get set, but when the gun went off, something changed in me. I wasn't that athlete who was calculating, who was patient to let his race pattern unfold, who strategized as he ran. I was a different athlete, not the athlete I wanted to be. I was more focused on my body and trying to get it across the line, shutting my mind down. I ran as if I were just competing. I wasn't sprinting. I wasn't strategizing.

As I got closer to the finish line, I was striding and striding. I knew this was going to be an epic race. Maybe ten meters before the finish line, I hit a flat step and stumbled forward. I wanted to get to that finish line before Usain so badly. But the big guy just outran me. He won by the slimmest of margins. He ran 9.79, and I ran 9.80. Only one-tenth of a second split us apart. Usain came across that finish line, slowed down, and struck his iconic pose. Then he looked back at me, but not to taunt me. Instead, the look on his face said, "Bro, this was yours for the winning."

Like any person would in that situation, I just wanted to hide under a rock. It was one of the most embarrassing moments of my career. The first thing I do after a race, win or lose, is find my parents in the stands because that's my "thank you" to them for bringing me into this world and allowing me to be me. As I embraced my mom, she could tell I was becoming emotional. I wanted to cry so badly. She whispered in my ear as dozens of fans crowded around us, "That's not you. Don't you do this. You're going to win some, and you're going to lose some, but you keep your head up."

So, I held back those tears. I clenched my jaw and put a big smile on my face. Then I walked around the stadium and waved to the crowd. But as in the press conference afterward, I still felt like crying. I was so disappointed in myself for running a race that I normally would not run. I didn't know who I was. I was happy when the press conference was over because I didn't have to wear this big smile on my face anymore and be very gracious and say things like, "Well, today wasn't my day. Today was Usain's day. He ran a great race today."

I left the press conference, walked through the corridors of the stadium to my service car, and went back to the hotel. Then I called my mom and my girlfriend and cried like a baby because I knew I had failed. It hurt so badly. I didn't know how to even approach my coach or my teammates because I felt like I'd let myself, them, and America down. I was supposed to be the one to slay the giant. I was supposed to be the one to bring home the gold, and I didn't.

When it was time to run the 200 meters, I felt hollow. I had another opportunity to go out there and beat Usain Bolt and win a gold medal at the World Championships in 2015. But knowing that the opportunity had already escaped me in the 100 and the 200 was a better race for him, I was already mentally defeated. And that's just how it unfolded. A confident Bolt and a hollow Justin went one-two again. So, I came away from the World Championships yet again with another double-stroke.

As I prepared for the relay, I said, "This is our opportunity, our chance to be able to win a gold medal at this World Championships."

To give a little backstory, there's a running joke that Team USA is cursed and can never win a relay. And it seemed like this curse was true, especially at this World Championships. We got off to a good start, but on the third handoff, the fourth leg left a little early, delaying the process of getting the stick around. And in grand fashion, Usain Bolt, the fourth leg for Team Jamaica, was able to grab the stick with no problems and carry his team to victory. Once again, Team USA had faltered.

I had intended to bring home gold in all three events, but I left with none. I had failed. I was so devastated. But I knew that the next season would be the year for me.

Before I finished my 2015 campaign, I still had to compete for the Diamond League Trophy. Yet again, I was victorious, and that was a win I really needed. I'd now won three Diamond League Trophies in a row, 2013, 2014, and 2015. No other athlete has achieved this. My 2015 season didn't go as expected, but it did end on a high.

CHAPTER 20

# Body Over Mind: Part 3

Now it was time to prepare for my 2016 season, which I was excited about because I felt like I had cracked the code on how to be a successful 9.7 runner. Running 9.7 had become the norm for me, which only meant one thing: 9.6 was on the horizon. I was ready to take that American record. I was ready to take down any foe in front of me. But even though I was motivated after having such an embarrassing season, my heart was still heavy.

During fall training in 2016, we shared the track that we trained on with a football team. They played football on the infield, where we did a lot of our jogging. But when the football team was discontinued, they took up the goalpost. And then the landscapers forgot to cut the grass, so the grass was longer than usual and grew over the holes where the goalposts had stood.

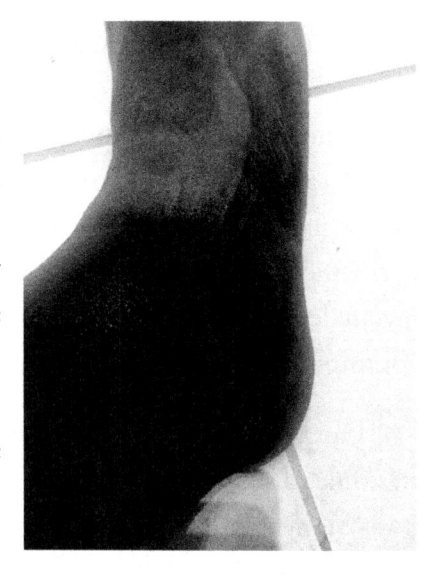

On the very last step of my very last jogging session, I stepped into a hole and fractured my ankle. As soon as I twisted it, I said to myself, "My ankle is broken," and I immediately thought my 2016 campaign had just flown out the window. Luckily, it wasn't broken, but my ankle swelled to the size of a grapefruit. I had damaged ligaments and had a hairline fracture. And it couldn't have come at a worse time because, two days later, I had to get on an airplane and go to California to shoot the NBC campaign for the Olympics. It was an honor to be called to be a part of the ads that they were going to use for the Olympics. I couldn't turn the opportunity down. They told me that it was going to be more like still photos and shots, where I was going to be standing and posing, so I felt like I'd be okay despite my bum ankle.

But when the plane took off, I knew it wasn't going to be good for my ankle. As we all know, once you're in the air for a very long time, your hands and feet start to swell. When I landed in California, I tried to stretch and test out my ankle as much as possible before heading out to the photo shoot. But when I got there, I realized that it wasn't a still photo shoot at all. I saw starting blocks, I saw a dolly, and I saw golf carts. This was going to be an active photo shoot. They wanted me to run, and they were going to get on a golf cart and drive next to me while I was running to capture more intense photos. I didn't know what to do. Should I tell them that I couldn't run, or should I go out there and try to be a part of this Olympic campaign? Using terrible judgment, I decided to tell no one and be a part of the Olympic campaign. I did a couple of starts out of the blocks, and my ankle and foot were in excruciating pain. But I gritted my teeth and got through it.

Once I was done with that, I packed up and flew back to Orlando. It was time to start speed and conditioning training. With my ankle injury, I was eating everybody's dust. Everyone was faster than me. Everyone was stronger than me. I was behind. I was really running on one leg, trying to be the tough guy. I felt like that season was playing with my mind. It was already bad enough that I was still feeling depressed from my embarrassing defeat in 2015. But now I was nursing this ankle, which was not helping me be the best version of myself. As with any athlete who sustains an injury, I wanted to cry because I felt like my whole world was over.

But I got through it, I healed up, and I actually won the 100-meter Olympic trials to make the team. I had bounced back. That was a monumental moment for me. I felt happy after fighting through all of that adversity to make the team and become, once again, a dominant sprinter for Team USA.

But Rio was a different kind of Olympics. Not only was I competing against tough adversaries, but the Zika pandemic had just broken out. So, being stung by a mosquito wasn't really in your favor. We were going into a combat zone where we were fighting not only against other athletes but also for our health, so everyone brought mounds of DEET, all of these different kinds of bug and mosquito sprays. Not only that, but the quality of the Olympic Village housing was terrible. Team Jamaica's ceiling was falling in, water was pouring down the walls, and some places didn't have good ventilation. In Team USA's building, which was usually the best building, the water system was not up to par. You couldn't take a shower for even five minutes without it flooding. You couldn't flush your used tissues and toilet paper because the pipes were too small. You had to put them in a sanitary bag.

And the food wasn't good, either. You would have thought they'd have done their best to serve Olympic athletes quality food, but no, it was more about quantity. The taste and nutrition ended up being subpar as well. Needless to say, I was dealing with all of these different stresses that I wasn't normally used to. So, while preparing for one of the most important moments of my life, the Olympics, a life-changing moment for any athlete, I was battling the environment constantly. There was no rest for me.

I remember waking up one night because I had no air conditioning in my room. I had to crack the window, which had no screen, so I lathered myself up in mosquito repellant, hoping that a mosquito wouldn't bite me in my sleep and make me sick. The next day, as I warmed up for the 100 meters, I felt tired and sluggish. But I was fighting. I made it through prelims. I made it through the semis and into the finals. I was as ready as I could be, but I still felt tired.

In the finals, I was leading for the first half of the race, but Usain came back and was able to seal the deal for his second consecutive Olympic gold. As I walked away from the track, preparing for the ceremony to receive my Olympic medal, it should have been one of the happiest moments of my life, but I stood on that podium feeling hollow and emotionless. I was still very depressed from the year before, and this year wasn't getting any better.

Now it was time to prepare for the 200 meters, but I still felt fatigued. The environment had tapped me out. Before stepping onto that track early that morning for the first round of the 200s, I told my coach, "I'm tired. I'll give you what I've got, but I don't think I have a lot left." I ended up making it through the prelims, but I did not get past the semis and into the finals. I'd given all I had, but I was exhausted, so I just sat and watched the 200-meter finals from the stands.

My last event was the 4x100, and that was what I had to focus on now. We had a great opportunity to snag that victory and finally break the relay curse. Mike Rogers was the first leg, and he had to hand the stick off to me down the backstretch, as I was the second leg. I did my part and handed the stick off to the third leg, who handed it off to the fourth leg. When our fourth leg came across the finish line first, I was content. I felt like the curse had been broken.

Not long after, while we were celebrating and high-fiving each other, we got a message that Team USA had been disqualified. Mike Rogers had handed the baton too early to me. Mind you, we were a threat to a lot of other countries, so we were always under a microscope. They were always looking to see how they could disqualify us, how they could play mind games with us, and how they could take us out of our zone. That was what happened that day. Ironically, the rule that disqualified us in 2016 was changed in 2017. I was furious.

After that Olympics, I didn't feel like Justin Gatlin at all. So, as I started preparing for my 2017 campaign, I was looking for a little glimmer of hope and light. This was hard to do because of the ankle injury that I had sustained. Now it was causing other injuries and complications in my hip, which was preventing me from being the rocket starter I usually was and was trying to get back to being. But I was determined to bring Justin Gatlin back.

Finding consistency in your process and practice is the first element to success, but to sustain it you need to be able to evolve the nature of that consistency. None of your wins will be the same or feel the same because the circumstances surrounding your win and the journey to get there are always fluctuating and changing. You want to operate at a standard that you believe is the one to beat, never settling for your previous best. That is ambition, the hunger and obsession that I mentioned to you at the end of Birth of Speed: Part 5. It is okay to acknowledge a win, but do not allow it to become an excuse to settle for less than your best. Not being balanced caused me to have two seasons, where I felt they were failures in my eyes. Although the world would see them as success, I sold myself short by not being at the level of balance that I had practiced. Even though I knew my success made me arguably the best in the world, I knew my best was better, and you should know this too. Your best should consistently be better each time. You should always lean on growth.

Follow my **Best Practices** below to always be elevating yourself to new heights:

- What is your beacon?
    - Remember a time when you had a win and felt unstoppable.
    - Relive that moment in your mind and the steps you took to get there.
    - That is your beacon that you can always recall to help set you up for success from a physical, emotional, and mindset standpoint.

- Don't forget how to survive.
    - Never forget what it took for you to win and thrive.
    - Remind yourself of that blueprint you used to reach success.
    - Always be open and searching for ways to perfect your blueprint along the way.

CHAPTER 21

# Climbing Mount Everest Twice: Part 1

As I prepared for 2017, I was still having complications. Even though my ankle was pretty much healed, my hip started giving me issues from being overworked. This made my start very inconsistent. Sometimes, I'd have a good start, and sometimes it would just be bad. Being in that crouched position and then popping up out of it is a very difficult thing to do to begin with, but to do it with one good hip felt impossible sometimes. But I was determined to bounce back and face these adversities for myself, my family, and my country.

This season, I started to show my age. Not physically, but in the sense that the passing of the torch from one American sprinter to another was on the horizon. In walked Christian Coleman, a young gun who followed in my footsteps but who also created his own path. He came from the University of Tennessee just like I did, and while there, he'd broken a lot of records and run a lot of fast times. Christian and I never had any ill will toward one another. I would talk to him before the big races he had in college and tell him, "These are the moments you need to capture. These are the moments that are going to get you noticed in the world. You cannot falter. You have to be great." And he would go out there and succeed.

Some would say I helped create a monster, but I don't think so because, at the end of the day, that is what track and field is all about: preserving the quality of excellence at a high level. When you're a sprinter at the top of your game, you never pass the torch. The torch has to be taken from you by a great successor. Maybe this kid was that great successor. If he was, I wanted to see. As the 2017 campaign got closer to nationals, the only real athlete that I had to worry about was Christian.

Before we lined up for the finals in the 100 meters to make it on Team USA and go to London for the 2017 World Championships, my coach told me, "Make sure that you are shoulder to shoulder with Christian Coleman at 50 meters and the rest will take care of itself." I listened to the plan, and I executed it precisely. It was a good race. My hip didn't give me any issues. I had to make sure that I was right there with him shoulder to shoulder at the 50-meter mark, and when we ran stride for stride to the finish line, I was still the dominant sprinter for Team USA.

Christian Coleman had declared he was turning pro right before that race. Now he was a professional athlete, and he was on a roll. That season, he had already run a 9.8 in the 100 and a 19.8 in the 200. He was definitely a formidable opponent, which made the upcoming World Championships unorthodox. In the finals, it was usually a showdown between me and Usain Bolt, but now we had a third. And we only had a month left before the World Championships, so it was sink or swim for me.

I had to create a whole new race strategy because my hip was starting to flare up again. And as I was running faster, it just took a toll on me. I talked with my coach, and we decided to come up with a different strategy but keep it close to the vest and not show the world.

With time ticking away and only two and a half weeks left, my coach, the taskmaster, Dennis Mitchell, said to me, "If this is what you want to do, you can't have any days off." And he meant it. I had no days off. For two and a half weeks straight, I trained every day. Hard. If I wasn't sprinting, I was doing resistance training. I was pulling sleds. I was pushing sleds. I was running. I was lifting. I was doing everything. I was rebuilding myself on the outside. But I knew that I also needed to rebuild myself on the inside. I needed to sharpen my mind and my hunger. I needed to prepare myself again.

When I wasn't training, I would come home and watch videos of myself all the way back to college, when I wasn't the best starter but had a great top-end speed. That's what I started to forge. I didn't rely so much on my start anymore; I grew more confident with my top-end speed again. A lot of people liked to look past the old Justin and say, "That's an old version of you, an obsolete version of you," but I didn't see that. I saw a race strategy that had been successful. Now I had to evolve, but I also had to rely on something strong within me and bring it back out.

Finally, it was time to go to the 2017 World Championships, which was behind enemy lines. I say that because Usain Bolt is loved and adored in the UK as if it were his second home. News had already spread that this was his last World Championship. That meant this was his last 100-meter race, his last 200-meter race, and his last 4x100 relay. When you're running at home, or in your second home, the audience wants to see you win. They want to see a fairy-tale ending, and I really believe the audience in the UK felt that way. As I warmed up, I could feel the heaviness of the audience. I was the threat. I was the guy who could stop this fairy tale from becoming the reality the world wanted to see. Now, by no means did I want to ruin Usain's party, but I was there to win, like always. To me, this was just another track meet, another championship, and another 100-meter race. Business as usual.

My heat was up first. They went through the roll call, lane one, lane two, lane three, lane four, lane five. There was nothing but clapping and cheering for the athletes. I was in lane six. When they called my name, I heard a little bit of rumbling, and then everyone started booing me. This was weird because I'd never experienced anything like it before. I thought that if I were going to be booed, it would have been in 2010 when I came back from my suspension. This was the same stadium where I'd won my bronze medal at the 2012 Olympics and received nothing but cheers and applause for being on top of that podium. The only reason I could think of for them booing me was that I hadn't been a threat then, but I was a threat now.

I ran the prelims like clockwork. I had a good start and finished the race in dominating fashion. But I still wanted to stick to the strategy that my coach and I had worked on. I didn't want to show Usain Bolt, Christian Coleman, or their coaches our strategy so they could prepare for me in the finals.

I warmed up for the semis and then came out onto the track. The same thing happened as before: the roll call of athletes, the clapping and cheering. But this time, when my name was called, the boos were louder and more intense. I couldn't believe it. People were actually booing me, and it seemed like it was becoming a trend. I thought that being booed in a stadium would be one of the worst things I could have experienced. Like being stranded in Europe or anywhere else in the world, boos were something I dreaded and did not want to have to deal with. But when I heard those boos, I only felt puzzled. I shrugged them off, focused, and regained my composure. I had to stick to the strategy.

I got in the blocks, the gun went off, and I ran my race. I had a good start, not the best, but I knew my top speed was there. Instead of pushing a button and showing everybody my speed, I throttled down just a bit, purposely getting second place. Once again, I did not want Bolt, Coleman, or their coaches to see what my strategy was. If I dominated the semis, they were going to know that I had a strong finish when it was time for finals.

When I got back to the warm-up area, my coach was puzzled. "What are you doing? Why didn't you get first? What happened?"

"Coach," I said, "I just wasn't feeling it. Nah, it was hurting me a little bit." I gave him that answer, and it was going to have to suffice. But I knew exactly what I was doing. I was confident. I was calm.

Up next was the semi for Usain Bolt and Christian Coleman, who were in the same race. The gun went off, and Christian Coleman had a hot start. He burst out of the blocks like a rocket. Boom! His signature move. It was probably one of the greatest starts the world had ever seen. As he ran, he created more and more space between him and Usain. Usain was not the best starter in the world, but he came down like a freight train. Once he was up and moving, there was no stopping the guy. But as he pursued Christian Coleman, he couldn't catch him. Christian Coleman actually won the race, but they both went on to the finals.

In the call room, I was picking up my warm-up clothes to put back on when Usain came into the room with a puzzled look on his face. He sat right next to me and said, "Who is this kid for Team USA? Who is this young guy?" He couldn't believe that there was somebody out there who could run with him and possibly beat him.

I told him, "That's the new kid. That's Christian Coleman."

He put his clothes on, and as we walked down the corridor to the warm-up area, we had a long talk. This was the longest interaction I'd had with him when it was just the two of us. Usually, we spoke with each other at press conferences, though there had been times when we were out partying after races, and he would DJ, and we would have a great time together relaxing and enjoying the "vibes." This time, he seemed like a different Usain. He seemed concerned.

CHAPTER 22

# Climbing Mount Everest Twice: Part 2

We had about 45 minutes to an hour before the finals. As my therapist worked on me, my coach sat there nervously, looking at his watch constantly. But I felt calm. I felt at peace. I was ready to go out there and compete. And with Bolt focused on Christian Coleman and not worrying about me, it took the pressure and attention away from me. I was ready to make off with that gold medal like a thief in the night.

We walked into the stadium from the call room, ready to race for the finals. Once again, we lined up for roll call. As they got to lane three, Usain Bolt, the crowd went crazy. It was like someone had scored the final touchdown, made the last-second shot, or kicked the final field goal to win the championship. They cheered for him as if he'd already won. The applause was thunderous. Right next to Usain, in lane four, was Christian Coleman. He got a similar cheer, but with him being the new guy, a lot of people still weren't familiar with who he was. They did know that he was a threat, though.

The roll call continued: lane five, lane six, lane seven, and finally, lane eight, Justin Gatlin. The energy that Usain Bolt got, I got in reverse. No cheers, no claps, no applause. Nothing but boos. It was such a thunderous boo that it vibrated the stadium. The stadium held more than a hundred thousand people, not to mention all the people watching from home, millions of people watching this moment.

I looked around the stadium and then dialed back in, saying to myself, "Y'all do not know who I am," because those boos were actually giving me energy. I didn't have to second-guess who was on my side, who was cheering for me, and who wasn't cheering for me. I knew who I was to these people. I was the bad guy. I was the threat. And I was ready to play my role.

As we set up and got in the blocks, it felt very foreign for me not to be next to my top competitors. I felt like this had been done strategically by the Federation and the World Championship Organization. Normally, the top competitors will be in the middle of the track, lanes four, five, and six, especially for television purposes. I was all the way out in lane eight. Usually, there are only eight lanes on the track, but this one had nine. To the left of me, in lane seven, was Yohan Blake, and to the right of me, in lane nine, was Reese Prescott.

But I didn't get flustered. I didn't panic because I couldn't see or feel Bolt or Coleman in lanes three and four. I dialed in. I used the resources that were around me. Yohan Blake was also known as a great starter. And I liked racing Yohan because he was a true competitor. Reese Prescott was one of the new athletes on the scene, and he had a high top speed. Anytime he won a race, he won it from behind. He would run everybody down. So, knowing their attributes, what they brought to the table, and what their weaknesses were, I exploited them. I used them to my benefit. I saw that Yohan was an athlete I would be able to race against for the first half of the 100 meters. And if I could stay in front of him going into the 50-meter mark and hold off Reese Prescott for the last 50 meters, I knew I would be in good contention to win this race and definitely get on that podium.

As we settled in the blocks, I could feel the body heat of my opponents next to me. We were not that far away from each other, almost shoulder to shoulder. The crowd got really silent and still. If a pin had dropped, the whole stadium would have heard it. All I heard was "set" and then a crack from the gun. Then I had nothing but tunnel vision.

I started running, and I thought, *Make sure you are in front of Yohan's leg. Run, run, run.* When I reached the 50-meter mark, I realized I was in fifth place. I couldn't tell you where Yohan Blake was. I couldn't tell you where Usain Bolt or Christian Coleman were. I couldn't feel them or see them because there were so many athletes in between us. But I stuck to my strategy. I didn't hesitate. It was time to activate my true plan, that top-end speed. But I still made sure to stay away from Reese Prescott by keeping him behind me.

After activating my plan and turning on the afterburners, with each drive, I picked off athletes one by one. When I made it to the finish line, I looked over at the rest of the field to my left and saw daylight between me and the finish line.

As I crossed that finish line, I knew I'd won. I wanted to let out a roar, but I waited because one of the most embarrassing things as a runner is to act like you won when you didn't. So, I waited for confirmation and just stared at the scoreboard. I also knew, once again, that I was in enemy territory. Anything could happen. I could have outright won this race, and they still could come up with a reason not to give it to me. But it was a close race. Christian Coleman thought he won. Usain Bolt thought he won. As we waited for the first name to come across the scoreboard to announce who the winner was, my name appeared: *"Justin Gatlin."*

As soon as I saw that, I threw my finger up over my mouth and shushed the whole crowd. Nobody in the stadium could say anything. I shushed over a hundred thousand people in nine seconds. The whole stadium let out a gasp. They were in disbelief because they thought they had ended me. They thought their mental warfare was going to do the job. They thought that putting me in lane eight was going to silence me and take me out of my game. But it did the opposite. It made me rise up to be a stronger competitor.

News outlets and commentators bashed me constantly. Even after this victory, they would still bash me to the point where other people would stand up for me and say, "Hey, this is a sport. There are no good guys or bad guys. There are no villains or heroes. These are athletes who have trained their hearts out for this moment, and we must respect that." A lot of those commentators were silenced because of their bullying, because of their negativity, and also because of their unwavering opinion.

The first person to come over and congratulate me was Usain Bolt. As he walked over to me, I bent the knee to him. A lot of people asked me, "Why did you do that? That was your moment to gloat. You're the man. You beat this guy when no one else could." But I realized Usain had helped me become not only a better athlete but a better human. He was the ultimate competitor. He either made you a better person, or you were going to walk away with your tail tucked between your legs. I had been up for the fight, and he realized that. Throughout our careers, we knew that if we were going to encounter each other, we needed to bring our A-game. Were we always friends? No. But did we have respect for each other? Yes. That gesture showed it right there.

As I came up from bending the knee, he embraced me and whispered in my ear, "Congratulations, man. If I wasn't going to do it, I didn't want anybody else to do it. You deserve it, man." I told him I appreciated him. I appreciated all his hard work, all of his fast times, all of his runs. Not only had they inspired me, but they'd made me a better athlete.

I realized at that moment that the crowd didn't love me. That was okay because it wasn't my time to take a victory lap; it was Usain's time. It was his last championship amongst his people and his fans. As he walked around that stadium waving to everyone, they waved back. They cheered and clapped for him. And I headed into the tunnel. That was good enough for me. I'd gone to war, and I'd emerged victorious.

As I was putting my clothes back on, getting ready for the press conference, I was smiling because I realized that I was back at the top of the podium again, and I'd worked so hard for this moment. But even in the press conference, reporters still took shots at me, asking questions like, "Why was this race so slow?" insinuating that something suspicious was going on. Usually, that would be the point where I would say something political to politely shut the reporters down. But this time, Usain grabbed the microphone and said, "Whoa, this is not what we're here for. There's no one else in the world who's running faster than us. And if they are, please tell me where they're at because they should have been in this race. As spectators, you should respect the outcome regardless." He silenced the whole room.

I was very appreciative because I realized that Usain didn't have to like me. In fact, he had the power to silence me. He had the power to end my career. He could have said, "I don't want to compete with Justin Gatlin, what he stands for, who he is." If he had, I guarantee you I would not have been invited to any of the meets he raced in—and a lot of meets he wasn't in. He had that much power. But I think he saw how determined I was and how hard I worked, and he respected that.

Ironically, my agent had spoken with Nike, my sponsor, earlier in the season about renewing my contract. By this time, I was a seasoned veteran nearing the end of my career. During the negotiation, he asked: "What if Justin beats Bolt?"

They said, "Let's see if that even happens." I think that Nike thought my agent was out of his mind at that time. But after everything transpired and I was victorious, they had to come to the table. Now they had to pay me.

But before all of that transpired, as I was going through prelims and semis and into the finals, my teammates would look at me as I was getting booed. The looks on their faces were ones of disbelief and hurt, as if to say, *How can they do that to this guy? How can they do that to him?*

I'd never caused any strife, confusion, or arguments. I got along with everybody. I embraced younger athletes. I was a leader. And I learned that I had to stay true to who I was regardless of the adversity I faced. I had to be Justin Gatlin every day, even when I didn't want to be me. This was a moment where it was necessary to be me. I was a champion. I was built like a champion. I fought like a champion, and I came out victorious like a champion.

**I need you to remember this:** naysayers are a part of true success. They are your sounding board for what is deemed impossible by average thinkers and doers. You will have plenty of times when you are surrounded by "yes" men. Those individuals may pump your ego, but they do not fire you up to prove them wrong. The extraordinary says, "I have a plan. A step-by-step process to accomplish the mission." In our minds, goals are like a to-do list. *I'll get there eventually.* In our minds, missions are critical and must be a priority. No one wants to fail a mission. So how do you do this?

- Allow your naysayers to ignite you.
- Feel that fire and turn it into your mission.

CHAPTER 23

# The Swan Song: Part 1

After winning the 2017 World Championships in London, the next couple of days were so surreal. I was beside myself. I'd done the impossible. I had turned the last two years of my track life around. The 2015 World Championships had been such an embarrassing moment for me, but the 2017 World Championships were a huge success. They showed my character—my true grit. I wasn't going to lie down. If anything, I was going to come back stronger and better than ever, and that's what I did.

Afterward, I went out to dinner with my agent and my family. Team USA thought I needed protection while walking the streets of London, so they sent a special forces soldier who worked for the team to protect us on our outing.

As we walked to the restaurant, people started coming up to me. At first, my parents and I were uneasy about what they were going to say to us, but it was the complete opposite of what we feared. Most of them congratulated me and apologized on behalf of their city. They said things like, "Congratulations on your win. I am so sorry. That is not the way we act. That is not how we were raised. We don't go out there and boo athletes at their most important time." This was said to me over and over again. You would have thought that I was the favorite and that London loved me the way they were treating me. They were so apologetic.

This was the moment I had been waiting for, where I could shed being the poster child of doping, where people saw me for who I was again. I'd worked hard to come back, shake that narrative off, and show everybody that I had a God-given talent, I had a pedigree, and I was a true competitor no matter what. If I was going to line up, I would give you my all, and that all was me. I finally felt like I was receiving my flowers, and it seemed like it came at a time when online bullying was at an all-time high. My victory was a smack in the face for a lot of those haters and trolls, and it felt good. I enjoyed the moment. It was like a breath of fresh air.

As I prepared myself for the 2018 season, which was another off year with no championships or Olympics, it was time to enjoy myself, have a little fun, and race at meets around the world. The first order of business was to go on vacation, and I did. I proposed to my girlfriend, and we went on a cruise. It was a happy moment. I was enjoying life.

But some people were still trying to derail me and defame me. Once again, they were trying to put me in a bad light. *The Telegraph* sent two reporters to Orlando, Florida, to figure out how they could catch me or my coach in an uncomfortable situation. They planned to act like they were working for a movie production company and were in the process of filming a movie about track and field. This made a lot of people excited because track and field does not get that kind of recognition. They knew that it would open doors, and people would accept them with open arms. They wanted my coach, Dennis, to train a movie star to become a track athlete. When someone asked, "Who's this movie star?" the fake movie producers would say, "We can't say. It's a secret."

Dennis took on the role, and I knew nothing about it until I got back maybe a week later. There were meetings about this so-called movie and movie star and how he needed to prepare, and an agent was involved who was supposed to be the liaison between them. His name was Robert Wagner. There was a situation where the movie producers brought up performance-enhancing drugs and how they thought it would be a good idea for this nameless movie star to take them to accelerate his progress to be a better athlete in this film. Once again, I knew nothing of the situation at the time. When this topic came up, it was being recorded on audio and video, and my coach became hesitant. He got up from the table and walked away. It was a situation that made everyone uncomfortable.

Now that the plot was unraveling in front of them, the journalists from *The Telegraph* made one more attempt. They came to the track when I was back from my vacation and asked to take a picture with me as if they were fans. The male reporter told me repeatedly, "My son loves you. He would love to get a picture with you. Can we take a picture together? It would be amazing for him." I obliged like I would with any fan, especially for a child I inspired. After they took this picture, they left pretty promptly, which seemed suspicious to me.

A week after that picture was taken, an article came out that said some sinister things were happening in our camp. The article told a sensationalized story of Dennis Mitchell being in cahoots with athletes using performance-enhancing drugs. Though they didn't mention me as the target or as the person of true interest, they wanted to muddy my name and take away that victory from me.

When this article came out, the hidden videos and audio and the picture that I took at the track with these two so-called movie producers were all in it. They made it look like I was a part of this whole scheme. I was devastated because one thing that my coach and I had always agreed upon the moment I came and worked with him was, "You protect me, and I'm going to protect you." We both knew what it felt like to be in a scandalous situation, and we never wanted to be back in that situation ever again. So, we held each other accountable. I felt like my heart was broken because he allowed himself to be in such a situation—and not for the fame, but for the money. As soon as this story broke, I had a talk with my agent, Renaldo, who advised me to start playing defense. He told me I had to separate myself from Dennis and this whole situation so it didn't seem like I was the bad guy again.

I had the conversation with Dennis, and we both were in tears. I told him, "This is not a good look for either one of us." I had to step away, and he understood that. But like I said, it was only for the moment. Next, I had a conversation with my teammates, and they understood the situation. They told me that I would return to the group once everything settled down.

I was so mad at Robert Wagner because it seemed like this was an intentional attack. *The Telegraph* was trying to derail my success. This whole plot was supposed to happen before the 2017 World Championships, so it could present me in a bad light and possibly knock me off my game. They were pulling out all the stops. But because they couldn't get it done before the World Championships and me being the champion, they felt like this plan still could work by assassinating my character. Unfortunately, this story started to grow legs and gain traction.

With a heavy heart, I began my search for a new coach. It wasn't that I thought that Dennis Mitchell wasn't an amazing coach or the best coach for me—we'd had so much success together and were coming off of what people perceived as an impossible win—but I had to protect myself. I had to protect my character and my integrity.

CHAPTER 24

# The Swan Song: Part 2

I went across town again and reached out to Brooks Johnson. In that situation, most coaches would say, "No. You left me. Be good where you're at." But he understood what was happening. Brooks was that kind of coach. He was not only a coach. He was a mentor. He looked at life in a way that a lot of other people and coaches didn't. He knew that he was a safe haven for me, and he wanted to protect me.

As I started to train with Brooks Johnson again, one of my old teammates who had retired a few years back, Rodney Green, was becoming a coach, too. What I loved about Rodney was that he understood numbers. He was able to calculate exactly what time you should be running by looking at a stopwatch and comparing the times when you were competing. He taught me things in track and field that other coaches weren't teaching, and he, too, became one of my coaches.

I was happy to have someone I could relate to, someone I'd worked shoulder to shoulder with, someone who knew how hard I was going to work. At that point in time, Coach Brooks was 77 years old. For him, traveling around the world all the time wasn't going to be an option. Having Rodney next to me on these trips made them easier.

But as I prepared for my 2018 season, I felt hollow because I wasn't where I knew I should be. I wasn't getting trained by the coach who had helped me become a champion in 2017. It just didn't feel right. As the season progressed, almost every other day at practice, Brooks would say to me, "You know you should be across town, right? You know you should be over there with Dennis."

I told Brooks, "I would like to, but that's not the place I need to be right now. You know where I came from, and you know what I've dealt with throughout my entire career. I can't have that negativity in my life."

That season went fine, but it wasn't the best. I realized that I was an athlete trying to celebrate his victory in 2017, but I was also an athlete who had been hurt by the ordeal I had gone through. I just wanted the track part of 2018 to be done so that I could focus on my personal life.

This was a huge year for me personally, as it was time to tie the knot with my fiance, Jeneice. Throughout the years she had become such a strong, loving partner and sounding board for me on and off the track. We decided to celebrate our love on 08/10/2018. We had a lavish two-day wedding with a beautiful mix of Hindu and modern wedding traditions. It was most certainly one of my happier moments in life.

At the end of the year, I talked to my agent, and against my own better judgment, I said, "Renaldo, I need to be back across town where I know that I'm getting the training that's going to make me the best athlete I can be." He accepted what I said and allowed me to return to Coach Mitchell. As for Coach Brooks, he understood and gave me his blessing. He knew I didn't belong there.

Leaving Coach Rodney was tougher. He and I were having a great time together. This was his first time being a coach, especially a professional coach traveling around the world, gaining experience and understanding. We worked well together. We were more friends than "athlete and coach," and we always will be, despite my departure.

I picked up the phone to call Dennis, and I started by saying, "There's no Tom Brady without Belichick, and there's no Belichick without Tom Brady." I used that analogy because he was a diehard New England Patriots fan. He knew exactly where I was coming from. There didn't have to be a deep conversation or a lot of sentiment. It was the same talk we had when we met for the first time: "I'm a horse that needs a stable, and you have a stable that needs a horse. Let's finish this out." He agreed.

So, it was a return to business as usual. As we prepared for the 2019 campaign, I had to work extra hard because I didn't have that full fall training that I usually would have gotten under him. The 2019 World Championships in Doha, Qatar, was our goal. That's what we were shooting for. I worked hard, I got back into great shape, and I won Nationals in the 100 meters. I was ready to run fast and run hard, and that's just what I did.

CHAPTER 25

# The Swan Song: Part 3

Doha, Qatar, in the Middle East, was an environment that I don't think any of us were prepared for. The heat was unimaginable. In the middle of the day, it was around 112 degrees. Thankfully, the championship was held at night, from 8 p.m. to midnight, for a whole week straight because at midnight, it was only 85 degrees outside. Once you stepped outside into that kind of heat, it felt like you were in an oven. It wasn't just the sun beaming down on you. It felt like the heat wave that blasts you in the face when you open your oven door while it's on broil, and you sear off your eyebrows or eyelashes and have to step back for a second before you pull the tray out of the oven. The heat was unbearable, unbelievable.

To make matters worse, I started coming down with something, a respiratory infection, where I was coughing and felt like I had fluid in my lungs. Then I started to get a fever. One thing you realize as an athlete, especially when you're competing, is there's little medication that you can take because a lot of them are on the ban list. This was a nightmare for me because I didn't know what I could take and what I couldn't take. So, all I would ask for from the team doctor was Dayquil because I knew that I could take that, along with ibuprofen and Tylenol. I was popping those things like Tic Tacs, trying to break this fever and get rid of this respiratory infection.

But I still had to prepare myself for the 100 meters, and the only guy standing in my way of being at the top of that podium was Christian Coleman, who was on fire that season. This was his best season yet. He was already in 9.7 shape, and he showed it on the track.

I made it through prelims, but in the semis, I almost didn't make the finals. I tried to execute the same strategy I had in 2017 when I'd conserved a little more energy going into the finals, but as I was throttling down, I let Andre De Grasse and Yohan Blake get ahead of me to the finish line. So, instead of getting first or second in my heat, I got third. I was in an unfamiliar situation. I stood there, waiting to see if I would make it to the finals. By the skin of my teeth, I did.

Now a lot of people were starting to count me out, especially knowing that this was the latter part of my career. I was 37 years old, a dinosaur in the track and field world. Whereas, usually, elite sprinters retire around the age of 30, like Usain did, I was well beyond that mark.

The finals arrived, and as we stood there behind our blocks, Doha leveled up their presentation. Before they went down the roll call for each lane, all the lights in the stadium shut off. We were standing in complete darkness. Then a spotlight would come on, focused on whatever lane was being announced. As they moved down the track, a holographic light show would appear with your face and name to show what lane you were in.

Once they finished the lineup, which was amazing, we got in our blocks and got settled. When the gun went off, I ran for my life like the Justin Gatlin of old, running his first professional race. I ran with all of my heart. Halfway through the race, I was shoulder to shoulder with Christian Coleman, but he hit another gear, pulled away, and was victorious. He was the 2019 World Champion. I was okay with that. I wasn't upset because I understood where I came from. I hadn't had a complete season with the coach who had helped me become a champion throughout my career. I also didn't feel well. I was super sick, and I had a fever.

Next up for me was the 4x100 relay. It was jam-packed with young, up-and-coming talent. I was the veteran, the elder statesman, on the team. I told the guys, "Full transparency. I've never won a gold medal in this relay in my track and field career, not just professionally but in high school and college. So, can you do me this favor? Can we go out there and show the world that Team USA is not cursed and we can win this medal and be victorious?"

They looked at each other and said, "We're going to do this for you, Gat."

I was happy. Usually, in a situation like this, the older athletes become a little jealous of the younger ones because the younger athletes are usually moving those older athletes out of the way. Those older athletes are constantly trying to hold on for as long as they can. Like I said, my feeling was that if it was meant for me not to bear the torch anymore, then younger athletes should take it. These young athletes were ready and willing. It was the passing of the torch.

As we lined up for the 4x100, I felt only pride when I usually would have been nervous. So much can happen in a relay: a dropped baton, a disqualification, a bad handoff, anything. But this race went off without a hitch. When the gun went off, Christian Coleman, who was the first leg, annihilated the field. Then it was my turn. He handed me the stick, and I took off. I burned the backstretch, separating us even more from the field. I handed the stick off to Jaylen Bacon, who gained even more of a lead on the third leg, and then he handed the stick off to Noah Lyles, who brought it home for us. We won gold. I finally won gold in the 4x100.

About an hour before the race, I lay on the side of the track, trying to regain my energy. I realized that I could have quit. I could have tapped out. I could have stepped away from that relay team and given that spot to another athlete. But I wanted to be able to go out there with every fiber of my body and get the job done. With fluid in my lungs and running a temperature of 101, I got my job done. As I jogged around that track to get to the finish line to grab my flag and embrace my teammates, I could see them on the big screen, yelling out, "Where's Gatlin?" They wanted to celebrate with me and be able to say, "Here's your first gold medal, bro," and send me off well.

Hearing all of the cheers, especially when we got our medals, was exciting, but I felt even sicker. I felt weak. I felt cold. I had the shivers. I had to use every ounce of my energy to keep going. A lot of the other athletes who were staying in our hotel started to experience the same symptoms. I didn't realize that something was going around. I thought it was a bad cold or maybe the flu.

CHAPTER 26

# The Swan Song: Part 4

After leaving Doha, I flew to South Africa, where I started a small community track team in Cape Town. I was giving athletes the opportunity to work together, not only as runners, but to represent their community, to do good in their community, and to give back to their community, all while going out there and competing as their community cheered them on. This was something I wanted to do all around the world, especially in places that didn't have enough access to be seen.

I stayed in South Africa for about a week, and my symptoms became worse. I would be outside in 80-degree weather, shivering while wearing two pairs of pants, two pairs of socks, a tank top, two t-shirts, a hoodie, and a hat. I went to a doctor and took any and every medication that they could give me to break this fever and get rid of these symptoms. Then, one day, I woke up and miraculously felt better. The fever was gone, and the symptoms were dissipating. I felt good.

After the trip, I flew back to America, and that was about the time when we started hearing on the news about this virus called COVID-19. I remember researching it and watching the news and seeing what all the symptoms were. That's when I realized I was one of the first people to have COVID before the world even knew what COVID was. I raced at the World Championships with COVID. I'd sprinted and run relays and won medals, gold medals, with COVID, the strongest version of COVID-19 at that. I'd felt on some days that I was at death's door. I'd battled through that unknowingly.

As the season ended in 2019 and the world began to understand what COVID was, a lot changed. The world shut down. You couldn't do anything. That left a lot of questions for sports in general. What did that mean for football, basketball, baseball, track and field, and soccer? What did that mean for a sport where you had to be able to stand next to other athletes and even touch them and interact with them? COVID was killing the sport. COVID was killing sports, period.

The situation became so crazy that they started to lock down places in our city where people could or would gather. So, no public parks, no tracks, no gyms, nothing. If you were caught on the street in some places, the police would come over and tell you to go home. It was that intense. The only places we could go to run were the grassy areas near retention ponds. The terrain there was so uneven. We couldn't even get to top speed when we were competing at practice, and we had to watch our steps when we were jogging to ensure that we didn't roll an ankle or hurt ourselves. We even went on bike rides.

Even when it became okay for people to gather outside, we still had to wear masks, and our coach made us separate and walk and run six feet apart. Sometimes, he wanted us to run with a mask on, which was impossible.

Our coach also made sure to test us weekly, and if you tested positive, you were exiled from the group until you tested negative again. No one knew when this COVID ordeal was going to end, and a lot of people were speculating this might be a turning event for sports. It was depressing.

This was a completely different frontier and a completely different world that really did not make me happy. This was not track and field.

As I pushed forward, trying to gain some sanity from the situation, I started to think about what the end would look like. My swan song. I read an interview with Brett Favre, a famous football player for the Green Bay Packers. When he retired, he said, "It feels like a piece of you dies." That stuck in my mind for a very long time, so much so that I dreaded retirement. I dreaded that moment when I would wake up one day and never go to practice again, never run another race, never fly overseas to go to a meet, never put on spikes again. Retirement meant the end of something I loved, which had been a part of most of my life—27 years. I had to come to grips with the fact that my plane was about to land.

I realized that throughout my career, especially in the latter part of my career, something needed to happen. After being suspended for four years and growing into a man, I'd gained wisdom in the second half of my career. I understood what it meant to be a champion and a veteran and what obligations came with that.

CHAPTER 27

# The Swan Song: Part 5

As we ended our preparation for 2020, the Olympic year, words started to spread that the Olympics were not going to be postponed. But they were. They were postponed from 2020 to 2021. It threw off my whole flow because I was ready. I was coming back. 2019 had been a great year, and I was hungry for 2020. That was going to be the year I successfully landed the plane. I was going to have a great career and ride off into the sunset. But then I remembered how Usain's career had ended, and he didn't have that fairy-tale ending. I realized that a lot of athletes wish they could have that fairy-tale ending but never do. So, you lean on the career. You lean on what you have done and what you have accomplished. Did you end up as a failure, as a loser? I didn't because my career was intertwined with success, with victory, with gold. That's what I would lean on.

The stress caused by all the unprecedented changes and challenges of the 2020 season came to a head, but in a good way. The birth of my baby boy, Jaxx, made all the stress disappear. Whereas Jace's birth turned me into a more determined athlete—fierce and ferocious—Jaxx's birth made me more human, sentimental, understanding, and loving. I felt balanced and blessed by God to feel this way. Getting through those sleepless nights was easy because of the overwhelming joy and pride. Now, it was time to refocus and get ready for the 2021 season to begin.

But as I prepared myself for the first round of the 100-meter Olympic trials in 2021, my heart became heavier each day. I remember waking up that morning in tears because I knew this was going to be my last Olympics. These would be my last Olympic trials ever. I was already mourning. I couldn't get it out of my head.

When I got to the track and started warming up, I broke down. I took a knee and started crying. My coach came over to me, picked me up, and said, "Get up. You still have work to do. You can't mourn something that hasn't even died yet. Get right." I pulled myself together and brought J. Gat back out.

In the prelims, I had the same rocket start that I'd always had before, and I made my way through in good fashion. Now it was onto the semis. But I had strained my hamstring a little bit, and I didn't want to tell anybody because I knew it was do or die. It was now or never. But in the semis, as I got out of the blocks and started to run, I strained my hamstring even more. When I crossed the finish line, I knew I was going to be in trouble for the finals.

This wasn't the first time I'd run with an injury. In 2013, I had a hamstring strain. I wrapped it up with an ACE bandage, and I went out there and still made the team. In 2016, I had an injury, wrapped it up with an ACE bandage, and rocked and rolled. I even made it to the Olympics that year. So, in my mind, I just had to follow protocol.

I tried to wrap it up, but before I put that ACE bandage on, the therapist wanted to check me out. He evaluated my hamstring and said, "I don't know how you're going to do this."

I looked at him and said, "I don't know how I'm going to do this, either, but we're going to make it happen."

I wrapped that ACE bandage around my hamstring, went out there, and got in the blocks. My start was great, but when I came up to accelerate, I had nothing there. I still finished with a sub-10, and a lot of people were amazed that I was nearly 40 years old and still able to run that fast. But as I came across that finish line, I knew it was a wrap for me. I was done. I didn't make the team. I didn't have that fairy-tale ending I was looking for.

I took my number off, gave it back to one of the young athletes, and walked down the corridor to the warm-up area. There, I found a little corner, and I broke down crying. I mourned. I felt like I had died. It was the end of my career. I was done. I gathered myself and walked over to my coach. We embraced each other with a strong hug. I kept telling him over and over, "I tried, man. I tried. I gave it all I had."

He said, "You've always given it all you had. You've made history over and over again. That's something to be proud of."

For the rest of the day, I cheered on my teammates. That night, lying in bed, looking up at the ceiling, I silently cried and said goodbye to track and field.

That inspired me to write a poem, which I felt was more fitting in this situation. I wanted to send a letter to track and field, so I titled it "Dear Track" to pay homage to Kobe Bryant, a huge inspiration to me, who wrote his "Dear Basketball" poem approximately five years prior. The poem goes:

**Dear Track**
From the moment I knew
running was a thing,
a thing that felt so right,
a thing that felt so free,
a thing that truly felt like me,
I have loved you.
From running around playgrounds
playing tag as a kid,
to burning down the sidelines
on youth football fields,
to racing the neighborhood kids on foot
while they were on bikes,

## READY, SET, GO!

my life changed the moment
I knew your name, Track.
With love comes challenges,
And you gave me so many
throughout my career,
some that were easier than others
and some that hurt more than life itself.
But through all my ups and downs,
victories and losses,
I have loved you, Track.
You gave me tears of sadness and joy,
lessons learned that will never be forgotten.
An unbreakable bond was made
for 27 years of my life.
You've given me courage.
You've given me wisdom.
You've given me peace
and a way to inspire others
to be the best version of themselves.
I'm grateful for our relationship
and the many others
I've had along the way.
The torch has passed,
but the love will never fade.
On your mark,
get set,
gone.
Love, J. Gat.

# JUSTIN GATLIN

# Conclusion

As I reflect on the journey we've embarked on together through these pages, I am filled with gratitude and a deep sense of connection. From the starting blocks to the finish line, each word I've written has been a step in a race we have run together. Thank you for joining me, for reading my story, for experiencing my journey, and for exploring the lessons that have shaped not just a sprinter, but a man who continues to chase his dreams every day.

For the parents reading this, I have something special for you—an afterword written by my own parents, who have been instrumental in my journey. Their insights and support have been my backbone, and I believe their words can offer you guidance and encouragement as you nurture your future champions.

Now that you have conquered your mountain and completed your mission. Celebrate!!! Take this opportunity and live in the moment. Reflect on how your mission has grown you. Be proud of all the work you put in to achieve your goals and cherish the process by making fond memories. Now realize how amazing you are and that you have elevated yourself by creating new habits from passion, discipline and determination. Take this wisdom and prepare for your next mission!!

If you resonate with my story and wish to connect further, I invite you to visit my website or follow me on social media. There, we can continue our dialogue, and perhaps I can help you sprint toward your goals. For those interested in diving deeper, my team and I have developed training programs and workshops that might be just what you are looking for.

> Thank you for reading my book! Scan the QR code to connect with me:

Once again, thank you for spending your time with me. Keep pushing forward, keep striving for greatness, and remember—the race is never over until you stop running.

Let's keep the momentum going. Ready, Set, Go?... *Further!*

AFTERWORD

# A Letter to the Parents of a Gifted Child

We are Willie and Jeanette Gatlin.

The very proud parents of world and Olympic champion Justin Gatlin. We say to all parents: *watch your child*. We say that with meaning: *you need to pay attention to your child!*

I told my husband I wanted to give him a son—a son born under the sign of Aquarius so we could all celebrate our February birthdays together. To the doctors' amazement, Justin was born just as we had planned. Aquarius is the water bearer, an air sign that rules over the legs.

My pregnancy was a very active one. Justin was moving all the time, never still. While sitting, I could see maternity clothes moving. Justin was a rambunctious baby. I would tell my husband that this baby was moving so fast it was like he was running track inside me. I was so ready to have this baby. My husband told me that there is a belief in the South that a baby will be marked by the tones, vibrations, and words spoken by the mother's voice while in the womb.

After I gave birth to Justin, the doctor held him, and he kicked and moved his arms so fast that it looked like he was trying to pull the oxygen mask from his face. This gave me a clue that he was going to be a handful. My son was given the name "JUSTIN" because he was born "JUST-IN-TIME," and there would be no more.

Justin walked at a very early age; he didn't crawl at all. He would pull up on the furniture and step off. He had no fear, and his balance and depth perception came easy after a few weeks. At eight months old, Justin was walking as well as any two-year-old.

Justin walked around our home, showing early signs of athleticism. It was a must to keep our eyes on him. He began developing his upper-body strength by climbing on all the furniture, on the floor-model television set, kitchen chairs, etc. When he was three, Justin would line up his toy trucks and cars in our hallway and then run and jump over each one. He was hurdling, but what did we know? My husband and I just knew that we had a very active son.

**Who Is This Letter For?**

Willie and I have written this letter for the parents of athletic boys and girls who wish to expand their dreams of becoming an Olympic or world champion, or whatever career your child desires to pursue. Pay attention to the early signs. Your child will show you who they are and what they enjoy doing. We knew our son was destined for something special, but what we didn't know was how he would do and learn so many things faster than the average kid his age, especially when it came to athletics.

Justin could not walk down the sidewalks of Brooklyn, New York, without jumping over fire hydrants, and there would be four or five fire hydrants on a block. This was Justin hurdling, running, and jumping! What did we know? We would let Justin cross the small street in front of our house to play in the playground. His favorite piece of equipment was the jungle gym. Justin was amazing, climbing to the very top and showing off his strength, balance, and fearlessness. He displayed agility and courage when playing tag. Justin was so quick that he hardly ever got tagged. Our house had a porch with about ten steps, and Justin would jump down the porch steps. By the time he was five, he had lost two thumbnails, but nothing stopped him.

We decided that with Justin being so physical and demonstrating such a high level of fitness and skills, we should enroll him in gymnastics and karate, both of which he excelled in. There was a group of older kids in our neighborhood, seven and eight years of age, and they were always knocking on our door and asking if Justin could come out and ride his bike with them. He could pop a wheelie as well as any of them. Willie would say Justin was athletically gifted, with no fear. He loved to be challenged.

Being a military family, we came up for reassignment and had to move to Pensacola, Florida. Justin was six years old. With Justin going into first grade, I became a volunteer class mother because I knew my son was very active and sometimes rambunctious. At recess, the kids would race and play all kinds of games. Justin was far more athletic than his peers. In second grade, he displayed more of the same athletic ability better than most.

Academically, I would work with Justin on his spelling words for the week while driving him to school each morning, and he always got a grade of one hundred. I also worked with him on his math, making him repeat his multiplication tables daily on the ride back home from school. After dinner, his dad would work with him on his reading and language arts. Justin had no problem with focusing when working one-on-one, but in school, his teacher said he would lose focus.

One Friday, during a spelling test, a bird landed on the windowsill of the classroom. All the kids looked at the bird and then went back to their work. But not Justin. He drew a picture of the bird. Once again, parents, PAY ATTENTION TO YOUR CHILD! Drawing was another of Justin's hidden talents. Justin began to ask for art supplies for sketching, inking, charcoal, and watercolors, along with an easel. His art was good enough to be entered in a citywide art contest, where some of his pieces won first place.

Our son's inability to focus became a problem in the classroom. His teacher called us for a parent-teacher conference, where she explained to us that she often had to tell Justin to stay focused. We were asked by the teacher and guidance counselor to have him tested for attention deficit hyperactivity disorder (ADHD. We did, and he was diagnosed with attention deficit disorder (ADD).

**Don't Be Quick to Diagnose Your Child: How does your child see themselves?**

It's a blessing and a curse when a child is diagnosed with a disorder. It doesn't necessarily mean that something is wrong with your child. Once again, *watch your child*. They might just learn in a different way, so be open to your child. Hear what they have to say about their feelings and what they are thinking. You need to ask your child questions and let them open up to you. Encourage your child, and let them know there is not a problem with them being diagnosed with ADD, ADHD, or anything else. We are all different. It's all about balance and keeping things in perspective. Remember, gifted children are still children. They just need a little help with being focused and doing the task at hand so they can move on to the next level in life.

After elementary school, everything went well. Justin was so happy to go to middle school for the first time. He was not, as he called it, playing baby games. Justin was able to interact with other children from around the county and community, and he showed off his skills and athleticism with them. Some kids were just as talented as Justin. They gave him a challenge, and he was excited by that because he finally had someone to run and jump with.

Eventually, my husband and I realized that Justin was excited about school, not because of academics but because he was totally focused on sports. Justin did enough to pass; he didn't give academics his all. My husband and I could see that his grades were lacking. Justin did not fail any classes, but he didn't live up to our standards. We felt we needed to teach him that life is not all about sports, and he needed to get an education, which is what school is for. We decided to remove him from all his sporting activities in his last year of middle school. He had to give back his uniforms and watch from the sidelines until his grades were up to where we thought they should be. He did the classroom work and was ready to go to high school with improved grades. Justin knew that we were serious about his academics.

The summer before Justin went to high school, he was offered a chance to join the Pensacola City League Basketball team under his middle school coach, Coach Lewis, who had an eye for budding athletes with raw talent. Justin had a long frame and long legs, which allowed him to run the ball and jump high. He is left-handed and was able to handle the ball well. He was also a very good shooter and hard to defend or stop. Basketball was just a fill-in, however, until high school began.

Justin started high school at Booker T. Washington, where he joined the swim team and football team.

*Parents: pay attention to your child and what they enjoy and thrive doing.* Don't lock them down into what you think they should do; encourage them to do what they like to do. Show up and provide emotional support. Justin enjoyed being on the swim team, but he kept getting sick. He left the team because of bronchitis.

Justin then turned all his focus and energy to football. At first, we didn't know that he had joined the football team. I did not approve because I felt the sport was too dangerous. I refused to pick him up after practice, so his dad stepped in and went to practices and games. The head coach would pull Justin out of the game, along with a few of the other freshmen, for some of the seniors to play so they could be looked at by college scouts sitting in the stands, even though the seniors didn't come to practice.

The coach had said, "If you don't come to practice, you can't play." Justin became disenchanted with him because he had gone back on his word, showing his lack of integrity to Justin and all the other players who had put in the long, hard hours at practice. Justin and his dad had a serious conversation about commitment, integrity, devotion, and determination. Justin said that the football coach was missing so much of what was instilled in him and that he no longer wanted to play on the football team. His dad told him, "In all fairness, you didn't tell me you joined the team, so I will not tell you to quit the team. You should go to the coach, look him in the eye, and speak to him about what he said about who plays and who will not play."

When Justin turned in his pads and helmet, the coach said, "You will be sorry."

Justin replied, "No, Coach, you will be sorry because I was devoted, ready to play my heart out for you and my team, willing to give you my very best as an athlete with all my God-given talent."

One day, while crossing campus, Justin noticed the school's track team warming up on the 110 high hurdles. He walked up to the track coach and said, "I could do that." The track coach then invited him to try out for the team. After Justin showed the coach his hurdling ability, the coach let him join the team. Justin won his very first race in the 110 high hurdles. After a few more local meets, he became a local sensation, with his picture on the front page of the sports section of the local newspaper. *Be open to hearing from your child. How you see your child is how they see themselves.* Justin came home beaming, and he told us that he had found his niche.

Justin enrolled in a college reach-out program, where he entered an essay contest with an essay titled "Unstoppable Teen," and he won! Afterward, that was the bar he set for himself; it was very high. Justin sang in the church junior choir, and he learned to play the piano and saxophone. His music teacher would say a child usually needed two or three lessons to play one note. Justin would get that first note and go to the second with ease. He was pretty good. Then came the braces, and that was the end of him playing the saxophone. That was okay; his heart was in athletics. *Parents, let your child explore.* We don't know what opportunities are out there, and just maybe, they will zero in on their gift.

After doing so well with the Booker T. Washington high school track team, winning over and over and getting television and newspaper coverage, the track coach could see Justin's gift and told us he had the makings of an elite athlete. However, since he was the only track coach for both the boys' and girls' track teams, with only one assistant, he could not give Justin the special attention he needed to develop into the elite athlete he could become. It was time for Justin to move on to better coaching than he could give him. The coach told Justin that he lived in the W. J. Woodham High School district based on our home address and zip code and that he would contact the head track coach at that school because they had at least six coaches and assistants who could give him the attention and training that Justin needed.

Justin told us that a track coach named Jay Cormier wanted to talk to us about a school transfer because we lived in the Woodham school district. We met with Coach Cormier and agreed to the transfer after he promised us that, while he couldn't guarantee us a scholarship, Justin would surely get a lot of "go-sees" because of his successful stats and raw talents. With the help of his coaching staff, he would turn our son into a world-class athlete. Coach Cormier also said that athletes of Justin's caliber and class only come along once in a coach's lifetime.

The local high school track teams in Pensacola would have district track meets. As supporting parents, we would go to them. I recall always seeing this same elderly couple with their lawn chairs at the meets. The only thing they had in common with the track team was Woodham High School, but no matter what schools were competing, this elderly couple with their lawn chairs would be sitting by the track. One day, I decided to stop and ask them, "Which one of the athletes is your child? Who are you here to support? I see you two all the time."

"Oh, no," they said. "We don't have any children going to school here. All of our kids are grown and gone. None of them live here anymore. We just love seeing this young kid, Justin Gatlin, perform; we truly enjoy watching him run. So, wherever the Woodham track team is competing, we are right there, watching and cheering him on. We believe in his talent." The real kicker is that after Justin was finished, they would fold up their lawn chairs and leave before the meet was over.

I could not believe that these people who had no attachment to Justin whatsoever were "Justin Gatlin fans." They were the beginning of the Justin Gatlin Fan Base. I didn't tell them I was Justin's mother. I just said,

"My name is Jeanette," and I thanked them for supporting the team and encouraging the children.

*Parents: know that giftedness is not an excuse for unacceptable behavior.* Assume your children mean to do the right thing. Point out what matters, and pay particular concern to politeness, manners, courtesy, and respect for others.

When a child is elite, whether it's in music or sports, they need outside advice, which usually comes in the form of a coach. At one track meet, one of Justin's teammates fell while jumping over the hurdles. Justin saw him go down, and he stopped, went back, and picked up his teammate. The crowd roared! They were on their feet. Once Justin helped his teammate back to his feet, he continued his race. Believe it or not, Justin went on to catch up with the competition and won the race. Coach Cormier was proud of Justin's display of sportsmanship, but he told Justin to never do it again.

**We All Have a Gift**

*I believe everyone is born with a gift.* Unfortunately, most of us go through life never realizing what that gift is. That being said, once again, I'm going back to the importance of paying attention. Watch your child; their gift is there. At one time or another, I would say to Justin, "Sit down! Stop running! Stop jumping!" But that was me. Little did I realize that I was stifling his athletic gifts. Children need the opportunity to explore life on their level. Whatever they show an interest in, encourage them to pursue it. Be a supportive parent at all times and try to bring out whatever gift your child has, whether it be academic, athletic, musical, or whatever.

Head Coach J. Cormier and his assistant coaching staff's recruiting efforts put together a formidable team that would win the Meet of Champions in Mobile, Alabama, and then go on to win the District

Championship of Escambia County. This propelled the Mighty Titans of the Woodham High School track team to the regional conference in Tallahassee, Florida. The Mighty Titans track team members did their research and understood that the school district hadn't won a state championship in 32 years. It was at this point Justin stepped up and took on a leadership role, displaying allegiance, integrity, willingness, devotion, and determination. The bar Justin set for himself after writing "Unstoppable Teen" was high. He won at all those meets, and the track team was very successful. In fact, he became one of the most sensational athletes in the district.

The track team won the regional, which qualified them for the state championship in Gainesville, Florida. Only six team members qualified: a high jumper, 110 hurdler, 300m hurdler, 100m runner, discus thrower, and shot put thrower. Justin competed in five of the scheduled events. After winning a few events back to back, he was on the award podium, receiving his gold medal, when he had to jump off and run over to the starting line to compete in the next event. This happened in three events. At the end of the meet, the W. J. Woodham High School Titans beat the best track team (Lincoln High School) in the state by half a point. Justin scored 36 of Woodham's 50.5 points.

This was a huge win for the six athletes and Coach Cormier. "The Gift gave us the win that allowed the Woodham High School Titans to bring the state championship title back to Pensacola after 32 years," said Head Coach Cormier.

**Drive and Determination**

Know that your child's perseverance, determination, and willingness to build up good stats will help them get looked at by college scouts and be recommended by their coach when colleges come calling. Justin amassed a very stellar track and field resume in the National Track and Field Database. Coach Cormier recommended that Justin compete in the Junior Olympics in Kissimmee, Florida. We agreed, but when it was time to register, Justin wanted to fill out the forms on his own. Though only a sophomore, he signed up to compete against high school seniors and college freshmen. Despite the age difference, he placed second in the 100m and third in the 110 hurdles.

After the meet was over, three gentlemen associated with the Olympics came over to congratulate Justin. They inquired about his age, and when they found out he was just a sophomore in high school but competing against much older, stronger, and more experienced athletes, they were amazed. One said, "I'm going to remember this kid's name," and another said, "I know I will see and hear about him again! He's an excellent athlete with no fear of lining up against such a stellar field of older, more experienced athletes. He's going to be a champion."

We thanked them for their encouragement, and as a concerned mother, I read the registration forms and became upset with Justin and his father. "Why did you guys register Justin to compete against older athletes?"

Justin replied, "I wanted to see if I had what it took to compete against stronger and more experienced athletes and if this is my calling and it's what I really want to do. I knew I loved track and field, but I had to test myself. No one else could give me that answer. My wins today confirmed for me that this is what I want to do."

**You Are Making an Investment in Your Child**

Find positive characteristics in your child and continue to emphasize them, even if you have to mention the good things ten times as often as needed. Justin's remarkable track record got him an invite to the

GMAC/Foot Locker Invitational at the University of North Carolina. He would be running against high school seniors and college athletes from across the nation who were very good. That showed us that Justin was a true athlete in track and field and this was what he loved to do.

While registering, Justin was told that he would be competing using hurdles at the college and professional height of 42 inches, not the usual high school height of 39 inches. Justin was unsure for the first time if he could hurdle this height, as he had never done it before. He told his father and me that we had driven him this long distance, so he wasn't going to let us and himself down without at least trying.

Justin felt the need to call Coach Cormier, who told him, "You got this! Go out there and give it your all. Get some rest and eat yourself some protein." Justin told us he wanted to go to IHOP for steak and eggs. Then he got some rest. Justin was ready for the meet the next day, and he ran his heart out. He ended up doing very well, tying for third with a college athlete. With this meet, Justin was on his way to becoming a world-class athlete.

**Become a Pair of Guardrails**

As Justin's parents, we had to face reality. Our son was a gifted athlete. After looking back through the years of his fearless competitiveness, exceptional skills, and prowess as a quick study, learning from every practice, we decided that one of his parents would always be at his meets. We had a very good relationship with Justin's middle and high school coaches. We enjoyed talking to them and learning different things about healthy athletes, staying injury-free, and athleticism. We traveled with the high school track team from place to place.

Justin would talk about his teammates and how they teased him about drinking juice. It was a funny story. We forbade Justin from having sugary drinks. We felt that he needed something healthier than soda, so our rules were juice and plain water to hydrate. We learned that when Justin would line up in the starting blocks, his teammates would chant, "Turn on the juice," because Justin would always run away from the whole field. I really believe most of the kids on the team could have been called "Juice" because they all started drinking it! We expressed how very proud we were of him for setting an example for his team, and we encouraged him to continue to do so. To this very day, when he comes home for a visit, people here in Escambia County still call out to him, "Hey, Justin Juice!" That's who they know him as.

**As Your Child Becomes a Young Adult**

Even after your child becomes a young adult, continue to support and encourage them. Believe in who they are, and your relationship with them will change. This young adult will have new and larger goals, but a lifetime of support glues the family together. Your relationship will stay intact, and at the same time, your child will have the focus to keep striving for better.

Justin graduated from W. J. Woodham High School in 2000 and went off to college. How do you know what advice to take and what's best for your child? Many colleges heavily recruited Justin. Not all, but most were offering a full ride, four-year scholarships, based on his athletic ability and stats he had amassed.

We say to parents with a gifted son or daughter, know that years of athletic endeavor will likely teach your child to handle adversity, how to be part of a team, and to work hard even on bad days. Have frank talks with them about the importance of social advantages. Respect the child and their knowledge, which sometimes may be better than your own.

This was an exciting time for our son and for us as well. Recruiting coaches were coming to our home. One in particular was from the University of Arkansas. He tried to recruit Justin by showing him this big box that opened up to display championship rings. Be willing to ask questions. We were still looking to see what else was out there. Florida State University, Florida A&M University (FAMU), and University of Tennessee coaches came recruiting. Clemson University sent Justin at least 15 letters. He also received letters from Brown University. Justin was able to go on five college "go-sees" based on the college recruiting rules.

We thought Justin was leaning toward LSU, but his father was not that comfortable with him going to school there, as it had a reputation of being a party school, and also because Justin loved New Orleans and Bourbon Street. His father told him that he didn't want to have to come down there and beat his behind all the way back to school if he was found to be failing because of the lures of Bourbon Street. So, Justin backed away from enrolling at LSU!

For whatever reason, Justin was feeling Tennessee. It was not the most exciting go-see, or should I say, not the most luxurious one. Coach Anderson was the coach who picked Justin up, and he took him to his home. Justin met his wife, who had been an athlete herself. Justin felt that he had been treated with more style at other go-sees than he was at Tennessee. On the go-see at LSU, he had been picked up in a new, beautiful Jaguar, but this time, he was picked up in an old, beat-up vehicle with the mirror falling off. But Justin liked the coach at Tennessee.

Justin had always had a very good rapport with every coach he'd ever had. When he made his decision based on how he felt about the coach, we thought it was the right one. Your coach is your leader. If you have the right rapport with a coach, then that's where you need to go. So, Justin chose the University of Tennessee in Knoxville.

We drove Justin up for freshman registration day, and we had the opportunity to take a tour of the dorms where he would be staying. We had a timeshare in the mountains of Pigeon Forge, Tennessee, and we felt we'd stay for at least a week to let him get acclimated to the school and see if he was really a good fit or not. Perhaps it was just for us. Even after your children become young adults there's going to be a distance between your ability to keep supporting and encouraging them.

The first couple of days, which was a weekend, we stayed at our timeshare. It had an Olympic-sized pool, and Justin went swimming over the weekend. We used this time to talk about our relationship, knowing it would change. Justin and his dad played a little putt-putt golf, and we walked around and looked at the scenery. On Monday, he visited the school. We were sure he would come back to Pigeon Forge with us. Instead, he met some of the athletes that he would be rooming with, and he decided to stay. He was treated to a big football game between the Tennessee Titans and the Kentucky Wildcats of Louisville, KY. He was so excited, taken with all the high spirits of the large crowds and the student camaraderie, so we had to bring all his school supplies and luggage down to the school. We felt relieved knowing he enjoyed being there. He never complained to us at all about anything concerning enrollment, the small dorm rooms, or the students in the school. He loved it! It all worked out.

Leaving Justin in Tennessee was probably one of the hardest things I've ever done in my life. I remember crying half the way back to Pensacola. All I could think about was how far away he'd be. We were leaving him, but at the same time, I realized he was growing into a young man. It was time to let him move on. We knew that this young adult would have new and larger goals that would cause our relationship to change, but at the same time, we still supported him.

We would visit him, especially when he had track meets at the university. We met some of his teammates and their families, and we would get together with them, take them all out to eat, and just enjoy spending quality time with the guys. It was the making of good friendships and relationships. Justin's teammates began to look forward to our visits as much as he did. We went to many track meets and never went empty-handed; we always had a big box of goodies in the back of our car for Justin and his teammates.

One of the meets we attended was in Kentucky, and it was a big one, the Indoors National Championships. Afterward, we took the guys out to dinner, still supportive but from a little more distance. We also went to Alabama and Mississippi, making sure that we attended all the important track meets, like the Southeastern Conference and National Championships. We knew that Justin and Leonard Scott were the jewels of the team, so we went to all those meets just to show our continuing support. To let him know that we were still there for him, we would let him see us in the stands, but we would keep our distance so as not to distract him or get him out of his zone of focusing.

Justin continued to call us and let us know what was going on and how he was doing academically and athletically. Once, when he first got to Tennessee and training was going on, he called and said, "Mom, I feel like an amateur. I've got to learn new stuff all over again, or a different way, or whatever."

I laughed and said to him, "Well, you are an amateur, so don't let that bother you. Just like you did in high school, you'll focus, and you'll be determined. Follow your coach's guidance, and you will achieve in college all the new and larger goals you set for yourself."

We often went over some, if not all, the same things we talked about in high school, which kept our family glued together and our relationships intact. Willie and I became, like I said, a set of guardrails. Justin decided that he would stay with Tennessee because he loved the environment, the spirit of "Rocky Top," and the bright orange uniform he would be wearing. He felt that he would be there for the whole four years.

We became Justin's eyes and ears, talking to the coaches, taking them to lunch, and finding out what they expected from Justin. We felt very comfortable with Justin's relationship with Coach Anderson. Justin actually became part of Coach Anderson's family. Coach Anderson and his wife had a young son. We were surprised when Justin said he would babysit for them. They were looking out for Justin; they trusted him, and they believed in him. Otherwise, they wouldn't have allowed him to be a part of their family. That was relaxing for us.

Justin was invited to dinner by a young female student while at the University of Tennessee. I don't know if she was a junior or a senior at that time, but she played basketball, and her name was Michelle Snow. Michelle had heard of Justin, and she decided to help look out for him because he was a homeboy from Pensacola, Florida.

**Devotion**

We had a lot of talks with Coach Anderson, explaining to him that Justin had been medically diagnosed with ADD at the age of nine, and he was taking medication for the disorder. We watched Coach Anderson at some of the track meets, and he was never still. He was a big ball of fire with energy burning in him. When we looked for him in one place, he'd be in another. We started to compare him to Justin's disorder; it was as if he had a case of ADHD.

Lo and behold, Justin fit in with all the athletes, and Coach Anderson was very pleased with him. Justin could be very focused once he came to the line; he never false-started. His pent-up adrenaline would be overflowing, and he was never still, moving and moving like a caged cat. So, we would always yell out, "Let's go, cage cat! Let the cat out!" Then we would look for him to come across the finish line first—and he did!

Back in Tennessee, at the university, the athletes were not allowed to have a car on campus during their freshman year. There was a time when Justin was homesick and wanted to visit, so he hitched a ride home with Michelle Snow. As I said, she was from Pensacola. Once he could have a car on campus, we purchased one for him, and he was able to drive back and forth. We were amazed that he took the challenge to do it, driving himself from Knoxville to Pensacola. Justin had truly matured. Our bond, communication, and relationship were still intact. We continued to support him and travel with him, and we watched our child, my baby, grow into this young man right before our eyes. *We are so proud of our son, and we will always encourage him.*

*To all parents with a gifted child: encourage them, be open to what they have to say and what they want to try, and support them.* You need to show up as often as you can and provide emotional support. Just knowing that we were in the stands at meets gave Justin comfort that somebody was there to support him, have his back, root for him, and show him love. It was also important for our son to know we were there for one reason and one reason only: him. Win or lose, we were going to be his support, and we were going to encourage him. We are and always will be his biggest support team.

We made many friends and met many people. A lot of people became Justin Gatlin fans, and they got used to seeing us. I'm thankful for that. I remember this one young man who ran with Justin's track team at Tennessee. I believe he was from Barbados, and he did not have the support team that Justin did, so we took him under our wing. We were his support team as well. Justin's teammates all needed to know that they had someone there cheering them on, supporting them, and being there for them. When we went out to eat, he went with us. We cheered for Justin, and we cheered for this young man as well.

The kids were good to us. They would give us University of Tennessee T-shirts and umbrellas with the university logo. They just wanted to show us they were thankful and appreciated us. They would always want to greet us with something, and I guess that was them being thankful that we were with them as well. We learned how to protect our children, though it was all new to us. As Justin's family and his guardrails, his two sets of ears and eyes, we learned how to protect him, be a close-knit support team, and pay close attention to the rules and regulations of college track and field.

**There Was Nothing More for Him to Do as a Collegiate Athlete**

After becoming the top-scoring track athlete for the University of Tennessee, Justin had accomplished all there was at the collegiate level. There was nothing left for him to do as a collegiate athlete. We were very aware that he was the jewel in the athletic crown of the University of Tennessee. As his second year at the university ended, we realized that the only reason for him to go back was to finish his academics. He had achieved all of the accolades, medals, and plaques that one athlete could achieve, including ten championship rings and helping the school win back-to-back championships two years in a row. Justin and his coaches had put the Tennessee track program on the map.

At the end of the college track season, there was a track meet sanctioned by USA Track and Field, and Justin was encouraged to participate by Coach Anderson. Justin had all the stats to qualify. This was at the same time as his final exams, so to focus and receive a passing grade, Justin took his prescribed medication for ADD. He just wanted to focus and pass his tests, and he did. All the athletes participating in the USA Track & Field meet were given a drug test, and Justin's urine test came back with minute traces of amphetamine.

We all asked, "What are amphetamines?" Justine's medication was not a stimulant. It slowed him down so he could focus and have clarity. It didn't enhance his speed. Justin was disqualified and was unable to compete, all because Coach Anderson did not check the box that showed he was taking ADD medication. Justin was labeled a drug cheat. This was heartbreaking for the Gatlin family. We told Justin to keep his head up, and that he had done nothing wrong.

We had a death in the family, so we traveled to New York to attend the funeral. While driving there, Justin received a call on his cellphone. All I could hear from him in the backseat was, "Nah. Uh-uh. Nah. Uh-uh."

I said, "Who the hell are you talking to?"

"Mama," he replied, "this is Trevor Graham."

"Who's Trevor Graham?"

"He's Marion Jones's track coach."

I vaguely knew who Marion Jones was. Justin told Trevor Graham that he should talk to his mom, and then he passed me the phone. Trevor and I talked, and I told him, "We are on our way to New York to attend a family funeral, and if you're interested in our son Justin, you'll respect our wishes and call us back once we return home to Pensacola." Then I hung up the phone. That was the beginning of Justin's professional athletic adventure. Mind you, we knew nothing about the professional side of track and field.

*Now, we really want to reiterate to all parents that you need to understand how your gifted child's life is going to change, and yours as a parent will as well, when they are elite athletes.* As the parent of a young boy or girl with the potential to go to the Olympics, you have to be as devoted and committed as them. You have to go into it with your eyes and ears wide open to learn how to protect your young and inexperienced athlete in every aspect of sports. This was a hard lesson to learn. It would be great for parents to understand the ups and downs, the ins and outs, and not have to experience a lot of the negative, nasty, ugly trials and tribulations we went through.

After returning home from New York City, Trevor Graham called and said he was a coach calling on behalf of Nike. After the debacle with Coach Anderson not checking the correct box on Justin's registration form, Justin had had enough and decided to turn pro. He was offered a great contract with very good benefits and was one of the first and youngest athletes to turn pro after just two years in college. This was in the fall of 2003.

We moved Justin from the University of Tennessee to Raleigh, North Carolina. At that time, we had a long face-to-face conversation with Coach Graham, who promised us that he would take care of our son as if he were his own. This was after the head of Nike Track and Field came to our home to close the deal. All of this was done with us beside Justin every step of the way. Nike recognized Justin as a young phenom and wanted him to represent their brand. We realized that we were dealing with a worldwide corporation, so we had to really harden our guardrails while supporting our son.

In 2004, Justin competed in his first race as a professional athlete in the city he was born in, New York. Justin came in second place at the very famous Millrose Game at Madison Square Garden against a lineup of well-seasoned professional athletes. Justin ran many races in the spring of 2004, with more wins than losses.

That summer was the Olympic Games in Athens, Greece. We were so excited to support our son in his dream of competing in the Olympics! Not to win! Just to compete at the Olympics! This was very, very special for him because Athens was the birthplace of the Olympics. Most of the track and field analysts counted Justin out, never considering this unseasoned 21-year-old sprinter a threat to win against such a field of experienced athletes from all around the world. Justin shocked everyone, winning GOLD in the 100m in the most-watched event on the biggest athletic stage in the world! As his parents, all we could do was cry happy, supportive tears! Justin came home with three medals: GOLD, SILVER, and BRONZE.

Justin's first year as a professional athlete was celebrated with a parade in his hometown of Pensacola. The celebration included his family, friends, Nike Headquarters staff, his agent, the mayor of Pensacola, who bestowed the key to the city, television announcers, high school coaches, and newspaper columnists. All came to celebrate Justin Gatlin, the hometown sports hero! Some of these people had followed our son's career from high school through college and now as a professional athlete.

In 2005, Justin went to the World Championships at the top of his game. He'd been deemed the fastest man in the world! Once more, in Helsinki, Finland, Justin showed the world his gift, his God-given talent, winning gold in the 100m and 200m sprints. We had always known he was a gifted athlete, and now the whole world knew it as well.

Just as the 2006 Outdoor Track and Field season was about to begin, and feeling like he was on top of the world after winning two golds at the 2005 World Championships, Justin was asked to support a dying track meet in Kansas City. Justin was more than happy to help by lending his name and making an appearance, and he also refused any payments. As his guardrail, we didn't attend this one meet, and not in our wildest imagination did we or anyone else think that another Nike employee would sabotage him by applying a banned substance to his body, causing a positive drug test.

The medical report said Justin had not eaten, drunk, or inhaled the substance. The positive test had come from a topical cream applied to the body. The only way that could have occurred was by the hands of the Nike massage therapist who worked the meet and was unhappy that Justin did not "bonus" him as per Nike's orders.

Justin had won gold, silver, and bronze medals in the 2004 Olympics in Athens, and he'd won double gold in the 100 and 200 meters at the World Championships in Helsinki in 2005. In 2006, he'd broken the world record in Doha, Qatar, in the 100m, winning gold. Justin had won championships for two years in a row; he did not need to cheat, not for money or glory. It was time to get legal counsel. Taking on the USADA, WADA, USATF, and IAAF is an uphill battle. You have to fight them one at a time, but they fight you jointly!

It was hell! The first lawyer seemed to be in it for the money and got little to no results. We received a call out of the blue from the lawyer who had represented us with the positive test in college. He said he wanted to help Justin because he'd failed to get the positive test removed after the IAAF lifted the ban. It was a two-year ban, and the medication that Justin was taking for his ADD was not on the USADA's or IAAF's list of banned substances. After six months, the ban was lifted, but the lawyer did not clear Justin's name. That is why the system called Justin a two-time drug cheat and wanted to slam him with an eight-year ban. This lawyer was too timid in fighting the system.

We had arbitration in Atlanta, Georgia. The ruling came in, and Justin's ban was reduced from eight years to four. A few months later, we were notified by the IAAF and WADA that they were contesting the four years; they wanted the full eight years! We had another arbitration, this time in New York City. We were told that we were under Swiss rules of law and, for all intents and purposes, we were in Switzerland, not New York City, and our third lawyer could not object to anything! One member of the panel was asleep the whole time. It was a joke! But the original ruling of four years stood firm.

We had a friend who was a lawyer in Pensacola, Joe Zarzaur. He was in New York, working on his own case, but he came to the arbitration to give our family his support. He told us that the case was so unbelievable that he felt he needed to do something. Joe has a personal injury law firm, and he came up with suing the USADA, WADA, IAAF, and USATF under the Americans with Disabilities Act. Based on the first drug test at the University of Tennessee, Joe's finding showed that Justin had been discriminated against when the system labeled him a drug cheat and banned him from competing overseas.

Joe filed our case in Pensacola. On the day of the hearing, all the organizations came with their lawyers. The presiding judge was amazed at the number of lawyers who showed up to fight our case. Joe presented our case, and after opening arguments, the other lawyers made a motion to settle. We accepted the settlement. Joe was the only lawyer who did not ask for payment upfront. He would get paid only if we won the case. Finally, this long, drawn-out case was over. But it had taken four years and $500,000 in legal fees paid out to the other three lawyers.

Justin returned to competition on the track circuit in 2011, and he showed his God-given gift by working himself back to the top of his game by the end of the season. THERE HAS NEVER BEEN AN ATHLETE

IN THE HISTORY OF TRACK AND FIELD who returned to track and field after a two-year ban and was successful. Justin returned after four years with great success and "slayed the dragon," the great Usain Bolt, in his last World Championship in 2017.

Justin Gatlin is the LAST AMERICAN to win a GOLD MEDAL in the PREMIER EVENT, THE 100 METERS, AT THE OLYMPIC GAMES!

As Justin's parents, "the guardrails," we stood shoulder to shoulder with him all the way. In the beginning, we insured his legs with Lloyd's of London for one million dollars! His dad was the one who took care of his paperwork, inputting his track competition schedule every 90 days and changes to his whereabouts schedule, which was mandatory with USADA/IAAF. I took care of all of Justin's finances, working with Nike and his agent, Renaldo Nehemiah. I also filed and paid his taxes.

We helped him buy his first home and paid his mortgage, monthly bills, car notes, insurance bills, and investments. We did all of this, from his first contract payments in 2003 to his retirement from USATF in 2023 at the age of 40. We didn't want Justin to clutter his mind with any of those personal responsibilities. We wanted him to just focus on training, competitions, traveling overseas, eating healthily, and getting the correct amount of rest and sleep.

As his parents, we will never leave Justin's side. We will always be his "guardrails." *We believe that being a parent is a lifetime relationship!*

# THANK YOU FOR READING MY BOOK!

## Scan the QR Code Below to Connect with Justin

*I appreciate your interest in my book and value your feedback as it helps me improve future versions of this book. I would appreciate it if you could leave your invaluable review on Amazon.com with your feedback. Thank you!*

Printed in Dunstable, United Kingdom